Awesome Atria Publishers!

Succulent WiLD Woman

Dancing with Your wonDer·Full self!

BY SARK

ATRIA PAPERBACK

New York ★ London ★ Toronto ★ SyDney ★ New Delhi

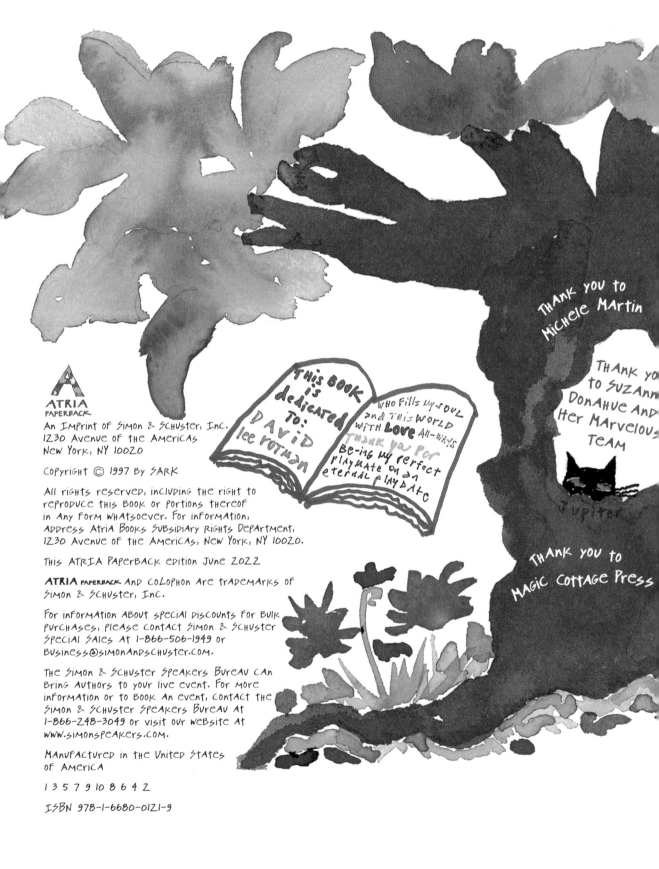

ATRIA
PAPERBACK

An Imprint of Simon & Schuster, Inc.
1230 Avenue of the Americas
New York, NY 10020

This ATRIA PAPERBACK edition June 2022

ATRIA PAPERBACK and colophon are trademarks of
Simon & Schuster, Inc.

For information about special discounts for bulk
purchases, please contact Simon & Schuster
Special Sales at 1-866-506-1949 or
business@simonandschuster.com.

The Simon & Schuster Speakers Bureau can
bring authors to your live event. For more
information or to book an event, contact the
Simon & Schuster Speakers Bureau at
1-866-248-3049 or visit our website at
www.simonspeakers.com.

Manufactured in the United States
of America

1 3 5 7 9 10 8 6 4 2

ISBN 978-1-6680-0121-9

THIS BOOK
is
dedicated
TO:
DAVID
lee rotman

WHO Fills my SOUL
and THIS WORLD
WITH LOVE All-ways
THANK you For
Be-ing my perfect
playmate on an
eternal play DAte

THANK you to
Michele Martin

THANK you
to Suzanne
Donahue And
Her Marvelous
TEAM

Jupiter

THANK you to
MAGIC Cottage Press

SUCCULENT:

ripe. Juicy. Whole. round. exuberant. Wild. rich. Wide. Deep. Firm. rare. Female.

FOUR BRAND NEW CHAPTERS FOR THE 25TH Anniversary edition!

SARK's MAGICAl Letter To You

Your GLOWING invitation...PAGE 8
Succulence is POWERFUll....PAGE 9
WHAT women want........PAGE 12
Serving succulence to
All Generations..........PAGE 13
A Whole World of
Succulence.........PAGE 14

LOVE STANDS TALL

SARK's time transporter...PAGE 186
Love never Dies............PAGE 188
Deeply Grieving, Wildly living...PAGE 191
THe Upside Down PAGE......PAGE 193
Love Comes Again........PAGE 194

MirACUlous Living

MirAcle MethoDs...........PAGE 197
CreAting mentAl weAlth...PAGE 201
MicroMovement MirAcles...PAGE 202
CreAting Sweetnesses...PAGE 204
Turning the Perfectionist
DiAl Down.............PAGE 206

Succulent Wise Women

THe Opposite of OLD is New...PAGE 207
COMPAssionAte Inclusivity...PAGE 208
SPArkling when things
feel AwfUl.............PAGE 209
CAlling All spiritUAl
AlcHemists..............PAGE 210
DeclArAtion of
Inter-Dependence...PAGE 212

Your Succulent

Being and Becoming A Succulent Wild Woman

Poster: Being A Succulent Wild Woman... page 16
Choosing succulence........... page 27
Living A wonder-full wild life right now!......... page 28
Waking up. .... page 31
(and then taking a nap)

BLOCKS TO Succulence

Ramblings of a dry and tame woman...page 34
How we stop ourselves.........page 38
Working with the hard parts....page 40
Investigating the darkness......page 42
(with a flashlight)

Fears

Feeling safe as a woman..... page 46
Going out Alone........... page 49
Being "self entertaining"..... page 52
Fear of being "too much.".... page 54
Old, alone, and succulent....page 56

HEALING

Importance of being crabby....page 59
Self healing.............page 60
Therapy............page 62
Healing places.........page 65
A room of your own.......page 67
Things to try for healing....page 69
Poster: How to forgive your father. page 71

OUTRAGEOUS Adventures

Adventuring without money....page 73
Traveling alone .... page 78
Adventures close to home....page 80

SEXUALITY

Succulent shy women...page 84
Erotic robots........page 86
Vibrators..........page 88
Brave wonderings. ....page 90
Sexual mis-steps......page 91
Sexually blossoming.....page 93

menu selections

SPECIAL NOTE: YOU HAVE PERMISSION TO READ IN any order, no order, BACKWARDS or upside down AS YOU WISH

Love and romance

Marrying Yourself . . . . page 95
Faces of intimacy . . . . page 98
the "Good Girlfriend" Must Die . page 100
lessons in love . . . . page 102
Living the process . . . . . page 104
MotherHOOD . . . . page 106
Hopes . . . . page 108

FAT

Terror of cellulite . . . . . . page 112
Tyranny of size . . . . page 114
importance of Breasts . . . . page 117
radical self-Acceptance . . . page 119
nourishment from the inside . page 123
WHAT Magazines tell us . . . . page 125

Creative expression

Journaling . . . . page 128
story-telling . . . . page 133
Painting . . . . page 137
Costumes . . . . page 140
MAKING Mistakes . . . . page 145
SHARING our creativity . . . . page 146

Money and power

How to explore Money . . . . page 149
How to Accept power . . . . . page 154
Living with Money,
Living without Money . . . page 156

portraits of Succulent Wild Women

Isabel . . . . page 161
Adrienne . . . . page 164
Giselle . . . . page 166
MARJorie . . . . page 168
Women's Friendships . . . . page 170

Building A Succulent Community

Succulent Wild Women Groups . . . page 176
Connected and in touch . . . . . page 179
WAYS to share succulence . . . page 181
Mentoring . . . . page 182
Growing As Wild Women . . . . page 184

This is your GLOWING invitation

To open your heart to more love, more succulence, more peace, and a wonder-filled life. Welcome miracles and your wildest dreams.

I invite you now to rise up, illuminated with love, and shine that love brightly, without veil or apology.

Let this invitation meet you right where you are, exactly as you are, unfinished and in process.

May any fears be held by your succulence and saturated with love.

Bring along any shynesses, resistance, or ideas of what you are not, or not yet.

All the feelings in your emotional family are welcome. Practice seeing, knowing, and learning to love them.

they will love you BACK

Know and honor your wildness as your intrinsic gift and feel your wild wisdom growing.

listen and you will hear it

You are enough right now to lead your dreams into being made real, and this is your inspiring invitation to do so!

San Francisco 2022

Dear Radiant Readers,

I wrote *Succulent Wild Woman* when I was 42, after finding these words etched into the cement on Powell Street in San Francisco in 1996:

"Succulence is Powerful"

Those words immensely inspired me and I jumped on the cement square in the sidewalk, threw my arms up, and shouted to the sky:

"I'm a Succulent Wild Woman, and I'm going to write all about THAT!" Then I collapsed to the ground in fear and felt sure I wouldn't be able to do it. I knew I might write words that would expose me, leave scars or stains, or hurt others.

I felt afraid that I wouldn't be able to write about my real life.

I felt absolutely terrified that if I wrote as vulnerably as I felt, I could never go back to any sense at all of "safety." Even though I hadn't ever felt safe since being molested as a child.

I knew that this level of openness would expose all of me to the world. Later I learned that true safety lies in expression, not repression.

I knew that in order to fulfill my declaration that I was a succulent wild woman, I had to try to describe my experiences of life as a woman. And I felt compelled to share the kind of stories and subjects that we don't often tell, but that almost every woman feels or experiences in some form.

So I began.

impossible means I'm possible!

I wrote and painted about everything in my life in full color. I wrote about fat and the tyranny of size, terror of cellulite, chin hair, vibrators, feeling like an erotic robot, fears of being too much, "The Good Girlfriend Must Die," the joys of traveling alone and having outrageous adventures.

I shared about women's friendships and succulent community, portraits of other succulent women, the necessary practices of boundaries, the importance of being crabby, creative expression in all forms, ways to navigate money and power, blocks to succulence, "How to Forgive Your Father," and many other truths of my life, and of women's lives.

I wrote about all these subjects so that other women would know that they were not the only ones having these experiences, and that our power comes from sharing about them, and feeling seen, known, and loved no matter what.

This book burst into the world in a big way. It was a catalyst for groups of succulent wild women forming all over the world, and it started a movement that continues to this day.

BOOK BALLOON

BUOYANCY WITH YOUR WRITING

Loving writing

SARK

The powerfull impact of this book came from women talking deeply and intimately with each other about what I had written about their desire to live in these wild succulent ways.

What meant the most to me, though, was that by authentically embracing my succulence, I had inspired so many women to embrace theirs. Many women felt that this book gave them permission to be themselves.

And I discovered that my fears had not come true. Instead, I was completely welcomed in all my most vulnerable writings.

and now I will never stop

I feel incredibly passionate about the power of women being themselves—really living their most succulent wild lives—and then sharing their full selves with the world.

I Believe thAt women now more thAn ever wAnt vibrant color, embodied purpose, creAtive Aliveness, Authenticity in Action, And meAningFull community. We wAnt to experience deeply intimate relAtionships, AbundAnt true love, eAsier joy, HAppier Bodies, more mirAcles, And the Ability to more eAsily creAte money And whAt I describe in this new edition As **mentAl weAlth.**

I Am inviting you, As Succulent Wild Women And leAders of A new wAy of living, to let yourselves Be even more wild, live even more AuthenticAlly, And join me in inspired Action. Let's shift And chAnge everything we cAn in this world thAt is cAlling more thAn ever for our love And Attention.

25 yeArs After I originAlly published this Book, I continue to meet And heAr from women of All Ages whose lives hAve Been trAnsformed By reAding it. Their stories Are full of mirAcles. They've pursued their pAssions, stArted or left relAtionships, heAled themselves And their fAmilies. They've Become Artists, therApists, life lovers, And used their gifts in wAys they'd AlwAys wAnted to. I'm heAring too from All the grAnddAughters As well As their mothers, who were given SARK Books By women of generAtions Before.

All The heArt·full people and Animals

12

Dr. Maya Angelou told me after I got to know her personally that "SARK books are cross-generational, like mine are, and they must continue to serve succulence to all the generations."

We Are Succulent Human Beans

and so they do

I believe Maya told me that because she was a consummate Succulent Wild Woman, and she believed in my vision of succulence and wanted to help expand it for the world.

Maya is now part of my circle of afterlife mentors, and I feel her wise presence every day. There's no reason to limit your mentors to those who are alive.

My mother told me she was one of the original Succulent Wild Women of her generation, and read this book three times. She is now part of my advisory circle from the afterlife too.

she wants me to remind us all to be gratefull for elastic.

I am witnessing women being more themselves and loving themselves more fully than ever before, and I intend for this book to be a mighty magnet for even more love and authenticity.

It's time for us to inspire not only ourselves, but also the upcoming generations of women.

I Believe we hAve the power to creAte the solutions thAt Are needed to trAnsForm this world into one thAt is more succulent For everyone. We will Do this By living AuthenticAlly And expressing ourselves Fully.

I First wrote this Book As my stAtement of self-liBerAtion, And I now see it As A liBerAtion of love For All oF us.

TAke these words And Art And use them in your own uprisings, And join me For collective power And chAnge.

I see A mighty movement oF succulent wild women uprising in collective power.

Giving and receiving unconditional
L o v e

I invite All those who iDentify As FemAle to join us.

I invite All the nonBinAry, genDer-FluiD, AnD trAnsgenDer people to join us. I Am so inspired By the courAge it tAkes For people to DeFine themselves And live in whAt they know is their true identity.

Consciously loving men who love and respect women are welcome in the land of Succulent Wild Women, and may we and our culture continue to identify and dismantle harmfull patriarchy and sexism.

I invite you to share the messages of this book, as well as inspired messages you receive from reading it, with friends, parents, partners, children, grandchildren, spouses, lovers—anyone you want to share succulence with. Succulence thrives on community.

I know that succulent self-loving women actively creating change are the power source we are all benefiting most from.

I've added new chapters of art and writing at the end of this anniversary edition. I've somehow encapsulated 25 years of wisdom and practices for you.

As we all join together in our true power and most abundant succulence, I am certain that personal and global transformation is possible.

Succulent Wild Women are powerfull.

Love, SARK

Being A Succulent

BATHE NAKED BY MOONLIGHT

MARRY your self FIRST promise to never leave you

BUY yourself GORGEOUS Flowers

PRACTICE extravagant LOUNGING

invent your Life over if it DOESN'T FEEL JUICY

CRADLE your WOUNDED PLACES Like Precious BABIES

Be Delicious

EAT MANGOES NAKED Lick the JUICE off your ARMS

DISCOVER your OWN Goodness

SMILE WHEN you FEEL Like it

SHOUT: I'M Here! I'M SUCCULENT and I'M LOUD!

Be RARE eccentric and ORIGINAL

Describe YourSELF AS MARVELOUS

WILD WOMAN BY SARK

paint your SOUL

investigate your DARK PLACES with A FLASHLIGHT

MAKE MoRe MistAKes!

WeAve your Life into A net of Love

You Are enough
You HAVe enough
You Do enough

Celebrate your Gorgeous Friendships With Women

tell the Truth FAster

end BLAMING

Dress to PLeAse your SeLF

let your creative spirit rush. FLoW. TUMBle. leAK Spring. BUBBLe Stream. Dribble out of You

Be inwardly OutrAGeous

Seek out other Succulent WiLD Women en. courAGe THe sHAring of MUtUAL TreAsures

Permission to Be Succulent

THIS IS A BOOK ABOUT CELEBRATING BEING A SUCCULENT WILD WOMAN.

It MEANS LIVING FULLY, RICHLY, RARELY AND REVELING IN ORDINARY AND EXTRAORDINARY MOMENTS.

it Gives you Permission, and CALLS you out to PLAY!

I Believe we MUST Live UNTAMED, JUICY AND ABUNDANTLY AS WOMEN.

IF we SHARe our stories, we will HAVE MANY telepathic COMPanions FOR the JOURNEY.

We Are All riding creative cycles!

JUST WATCH US ride!

MY OWN JOURNEY is FULL OF FEAR, pain, love, SHAME, WONDER, ecstasy, luck, DARING, and MARVELOUS imperfections.

I invite you to travel along with me as I share my stumblings, astonishments, and discoveries as a woman.

Whenever I read travel books, I am so grateful that other people go to far-flung places, climb mountains, join expeditions, and then write about their experiences. I feel grateful because I can vicariously travel with them

Without Having to Get out of Bed!

our dreams will lead us to succulent places!

we love to STAY in bed

Here are some scenarios to go along with reading this book:

- in A SHAFT of SunLiGHT, BeSiDe A BOWL of oranGes, BAreFoot.
- in the BAtHtuB with Many candles and slices of ManGo.
- in WHite cotton PAJAMAS, under A COMForter with A CAT sleepinG in A circle.

I write All My BOOKS LyinG DOWn in PAJAMAS and MeASure time BY MuGS of teA.

reMeMBer PAJAMAS with Feet? THe FeeT HAD little White BuMPS THAT Gripped onTo everything

MY lucky POLKA DOT MUG

I DO not Know More than you DO.
My investiGATions HAVe sHown tHAT
we Frequently think others Know [it]
But we Dont Know [it].

WHAT is [it]?

My younGer Brother, anDrew, Always
says,

"WHen you Give these tALKS in puBLic,
Be sure to start By telling people How
Many probLeMs you HAVe."

"isnt it oBvious?" I Always think.
anDrew says it's not. I Guess I looK
BriGHT anD untrouBLeD, anD I sMile
A lot, wHicH is soMetiMes A MASK
to HiDe sHyness, FeAr, or pain.

THe BooKS I write HAVe colorFUL,
HAppy covers, wHicH Can CAuse
people to think:

it must be easy for her

It isn't easy for any of us to transcend the past, or pain we might have suffered. Yet, there are gifts in those pains, and we can choose to let light into the dark places. We are not alone!

"I have woven a parachute out of everything broken."
William Stafford

I was physically and sexually abused by an older brother for about 7 years. This caused me to live in my imagination and to create worlds other than the one I was actually living in.

This also set up patterns of self-destruction that became addictions and self-hatred that persisted for many years.

I've written about the incest in my second book: Inspiration Sandwich in a chapter called "Transforming negatives."

I emerged from that incest to live a frantic and unconscious life, traveling and living with millionaires on tropical islands, and being described as

"The Marshmallow Venus."

I often thought that if men could walk around in the world for one day as women, and hear the comments from other men that women hear, they would rush to us in incredulous disbelief, and help us to form safety patrols.

I spent many years being furious with men. I didn't realize that they were experiencing oppression of a different kind. I had to have an enemy, a place to rage. I had many examples of "bad men."

I didn't understand that my own self-hatred was being projected onto the world, and how much I was playing the part of the angry victim— and sometimes still am.

Now, I'm surrounded by marvelous men.

After many years of self-healing, therapy, and investigating my interior, I bring you this collection of stories, memories, simple truths, and SUCCULENCE.

SUCCULENT WILD WOMAN:
A WOMAN of any AGe Who Feels Free to FUlly express Herself in every Dimension of Her life.

A note to young or not yet Formed Succulent WILD woMen:
STanD FirM and WHole AS A WoMan. You Are precious and irreplaceAble. Treasure your FeMAle self. CHoose innocence. invent ways to FeeL More Free. investiGATe your DARKnesses.

A note To THose who love Succulent WILD woMen:
learn tHoroUGHLy Your OWN FeMAle siDe. Support Freedom and releAse JUDGMents. Be SeXUAL only MUtually. let Go of FEARs. SpeAK respectFully. Spend reAL, intiMAte time with WoMen.

invesT in SUcculence

Choosing Succulence

I am not always a positive person. People call my inspiration phone line, or read my books, and decide that I'm this super-positive person with glitter in her hair and a beatific smile (well, sometimes it's true...). Glitter does seem to follow me.

Being "positive" is a choice. I am flooded with the same doubts, terrors, insecurities, rages, incessant worries, and critical inner voices as everyone else — maybe more!

Sometimes I go overboard describing my faults or flaws, to the extent that I see people cringe and wonder, "Why am I listening to/reading this person if she is so riddled with stuff?" We are all riddled with stuff!

I said this same thing to my therapist when I stopped idealizing him so much and saw his flaws. "You mean I'm just seeing a regular guy?" Or, as Elisabeth Kübler Ross says, "I'm not O.K., you're not O.K., and that's O.K.!" My positive self developed partly in response to the ugliness of the alternative. Some days, I feel myself sliding into a negative pool...

My friend Brigette calls this the "Sea of Bitterness"

Sometimes I just sit in a negative pool of my own making

Friends pull me out, or I catch myself.

In WHAT WAYS Are you tempted to collapse into The negative?

I feel it's MUCH More interesting to Focus on and MAGnify the postive. You can use A MAGnifying GLASS. The negative is still there—it's Just thAT the spotLiGHT is on the positive.

Many of us Grew up with A lArGe Focus on the negative. PArt of This WAS GenerATionAL, or Just HABituAL. PHrAses Like, "Just WAit until The other sHoe Drops."
"Don't count your cHickens Before They're HATcHed."

poor DroppeD sHoe

1 2 3

"I'll Give you something to cry ABout." "We Didn't Want you to Get A swelled (or BiG) HeAD."

Do you ActuAlly Know anyone wHo Got A "swelled HeAD" From too MucH prAise? UsuAlly, it WAs FAr too little, and they retreated to Their eGo For escApe and BecAMe GrAnDiose As A type of Defense. No MAtter How Dry and scAred we MiGHT Be, I Believe we Must CHOOSe SvcCvlence

Succulence next stop

over and over. Sometimes HunDreds of times in A DAY— or Thousands!

The negative can Be so seductive. You cAn usuAlly FinD someone to spend time BeinG criticAL, JuDGMentA, and DArk with.

DArk GlAsses

26

COMPLAINERS ALWAYS FIND EACH OTHER, AND USUALLY IN SOME
SITUATION THEY'VE CREATED TO COMPLAIN ABOUT! (NOTE: AS A
"MASTER COMPLAINER" MYSELF, I'M WORKING ON THE PATTERNS THAT
MAKE THIS FEEL REWARDING.) BEING POSITIVE DOES NOT MEAN
BEING ACCEPTING OF THE NEGATIVE, OR IGNORANT OF THE ISSUES, OR
THE WORLD SITUATION, OR ANYTHING ELSE.

It MEANS SEEING THE GRACE in AS MUCH AS YOU CAN SEE.

Like CLOUD WATCHING... the SHAPES WE SEE ARE CREATED BY OUR VISION

CHOOSING SUCCULENCE will ENABLE US TO BE MORE ALIVE, MORE
CONTRIBUTING, FLEXIBLE, AND FRESH. I ASK MYSELF FREQUENTLY,
"HOW CAN I TURN THIS AROUND? HOW CAN I SEE WITH SUCCULENT EYES?"
ALMOST ANY SITUATION CAN BE SEEN IN A NEW LIGHT.

A BRAND NEW LIGHT

"Tell ALL the truth-but tell it slant."
                              EMILY DICKINSON

CHOOSING SUCCULENCE is A DELIBERATE ACT of
PERSONAL revolution. It MEANS WAKING UP! EMBRACING
your TRUE SELF, STUDYING your PATTERNS, and letting
out your MOST ALIVE SELF.   WE   ALL   HAVE   ONE.

THE SUCCULENT PERSON is BURSTING WITH JUICES, STORIES,
ANIMATIONS, IDEAS, AND LOVE. THE DRY PERSON LOOKS
SIDEWAYS AND SAYS, "WHO DO YOU THINK YOU ARE?"

USE AN UMBRELLA to SHIELD yourself From this person

"IF YOU ASKED ME WHAT I CAME INTO
THIS WORLD TO DO, I WILL TELL YOU.
I CAME TO LIVE OUT LOUD."
                    EMILE ZOLA

Living A Wonder·Full Wild Life right now.

We Deserve Wildness. Wildness can Be As simple As wearing tall Boots when none of your Friends DO, or talking to Gorgeous strangers, or visiting expensive Hotels for just A cup of teA. Whatever takes us out of our routine and gives us A little interior spark, is Wild.

Being tAme is what we're tAught:
···put the crayons BACK, stay in line, Dont talk too loud, keep your knees together, nice Girls Dont...

As you might know, nice GiRLS DO, and they like to feel wild and Alive. Being tAme feels sAfe, Being wild, unsAfe. Yet sAfety is an illusion anyway.
we Are not in control.
As A controlling type of person, I HAte this FACT.

no MAtter How Dry and tAme and nice we live, we will Die. We will Also suffer Along the WAy.

Living wild is its own reward. Tiny wildnesses Are everywhere to experiment with:

Throwing All of the crayons out of the box into A Big Wild color pile

Dont stand in line At the Bank. Sit Down and reAD A Book. put change into pay phones in the coin return.

The change will come BACK to you in another Form

28

Sit with your legs up on the Furniture and DRAW inside your own BOOKS.

When my Boyfriend First read my Books, He went through and wrote to me in all the spaces and margins.
I treasure His murmurings.

Go Wandering! Let the world show you the most wild path. Speaking to strangers is an excellent exercise. Use your intuition as guidance and listen to WHAT you Hear. Be exposed.

Live A WILD, vulnerable life. Let us see you, LAUGHING loudly, WALKING FLAMBOYANTLY, and WEARING colors that Don't MATCH.

My Mother used to SAY that my sense of color was GARish — look At me now, MOM!

Dress like an angel and WALK A TIGHT rope

Let us see you celebrating in public, eating Heartily, creating BOLDLY, Dancing wildly or BADLY.

Sometimes I see women who look like captives. Dry and Hunted, they scurry from curb to car. They look too thin and not JOY-FULL. They Don't Go out unless it's with A Man, or to the "right event."

Like Blades, they are sharp and can be Dangerous

Go out wildly and Alone
or with A selection of outrageous women friends

Go out in All your own wild Glory

Living wild has consequences. welcome these and learn from them. please give yourself too many Gifts! So often, I meet women who say, "I really shouldn't be buying All this for myself..." why not? Don't you Deserve it? My Mother TAUGHT me not to wait for A man to buy Me Flowers. She Always said, "Buy your own Flowers, too." and so I do...
I Also receive them

Stop Apologizing and saying, "Im sorry" so much. women have a terrible Habit of Apologizing for everything (even their own existence). One time, I bumped into A woman—Hard—and she said Automatically, "Im sorry." I had Bumped into Her! Sorry in the Dictionary says this: wretched, Miserable, inferior in worth or quality. We Are not this!

We Have A right to live wild, succulent lives. right now. Open your window and yell At the top of your lungs:

"Im Here! Im wild! I will live A Daring and remarkable Life!"

We're Here!

We're wild!!

We're succulent! You can't stop us!!!

windows everywhere were flung open

WAKING UP
(and then, taking a nap)

It is tempting to sleepwalk through life.
To tell HALF-truths, listen HALF-way, Be HALF-Asleep,
Drive with HALF Attention...

WAKE UP!

We need you As an Alive and AWAKE Woman, listening
and contributing. WAKE up your Creative Genius and
let it out into the world. WAKE up your power and
use it wisely. WAKE up to your pain and investigate it.

Her creative Genius WAS A STAR-SHAPED Kite thAT Flew HIGH and FAr

WAKE up the DULL OLD pARts thAt Are HiDiNG From the
LIGHT. WAKE up to love and let it FlooD Through you.

love FlooDED in and out

WAKE up to see the other souls Around you. Let them
Affect you. Live in the center of your life.

"CLuster Together Like sTArs."

Henry Miller

now thAt you've AWAKened...

immediately take a nap! naps are when the angels come out to take special care of you.

The angels carried her in a healing hammock and sprinkled dream dust on her

None of us get enough naps. naps are essential for mental health. naps are productive—contrary to what we've been taught.

The more naps you take, the more money you'll make! it's true.

Our culture promotes tension and crabbiness. Part of this is the severe lack of naps. Declare your home, or wherever you are, as a Free nap zone.

I met a woman in her 70's who came up to me after a workshop and said, "Thank you for giving me permission. My back is killing me. I'm going up to my hotel room and taking a nap! I have never done anything so self-indulgent. Isn't that sad?"

Plant and fly permission flags
All over your life!

I dreamed the other night of music boxes hidden all over my garden. I think of us all as music boxes — beautiful and full of music... especially when we open up!

Being and Becoming A Succulent Wild Woman

resources

- Untamed By Glennon Doyle
- We Can Do Hard Things Podcast By Glennon Doyle
- Wild Women Sisterhood www.wildwomansisterhood.com
- Evolving Wisdom Dr. Claire Zammit, Ph.D., evolvingwisdom.com
- Girl God Books Trista Hendren www.thegirlgod.com
- Hiro Boga hiroboga.com "I Am A Business Artist, Mentor And Soul Alchemist"
- Patti Digh www.pattidigh.com

rAMBLings of A Dry and Tame Woman

I'm under "House Arrest." I put myself in this state so that I would actually write something instead of distracting myself in countless ways. I'm feeling very spoiled and self-indulgent and stupid. I keep eating things that make me sick. I keep thinking that I'll turn into some kind of "moderate person" who can have a box of thin mint Girl Scout cookies for longer than a day.

visions of thin mints danced in her head

refrigerate for Best Taste...

I start out with 2 or 3 cookies in a bowl (imagining that I'm a "moderate person.") Then, it turns into 3 cookies every 1/2 hour until they're gone! The only way I can really resist is not to have them in the house at all— which gets scary when someone gives me a gift of a whole box of cookies (But thank you angela!).

I'm learning to say "No Thank you!" But sometimes I feel weak or old, or in need of some vital comfort that I haven't yet learned how to find inside myself.

During these times, I'm still learning to give myself love and self-Acceptance. Admitting these things in writing helps. Learning that I'm not alone really helps.

Before I can really <u>Live</u> as a succulent wild woman, I find that I must explore the Dry, Tame, Dark parts of myself.

if she got really quiet and listened, new parts of her wanted to speak.

34

I resist MY DARK PLACES, and try to Hide them From other people, But MosTly myself. Sometimes I Just skip From one ADDictive BeHavior to another — WHATever is loudest, and will Most Quickly Fill the emptiness.

the Hole you can never Fill

How Deep is the emptiness? even if you COULD MANAGE to Fill it, WOULD thAT MAKE you HAPPY?

Sometimes I AM ABLe to Meditate and Go For A long nourishing WALK. Sometimes I Just lie FLAT and still in A DArkeneD room, FUMBLING For the leG of GOD to HOLD onto.

DID YOU
ever wonder
WHAT the
leG of GOD
WOULD look like?

One of the ways to Arrive AT succulence and wildness is to Allow the pArts that Arent. I will list Some of MY FAULTS and weaknesses in the Hopes that it MIGHT inspire you to DO the SAME. Letting it Be seen takes AWAY its power.

I'M CODependent, A recovering incest survivor and ALMOST an AlcoHolic (AAA!), oBsessively/CoMpulsively Driven, overly sensitive and HiGHly sensitive, suBject to pArAnoid thinking and MArtyrDoM, and I live lArGely in A state of DeniAL. My therApist MIGHT ADD: nArcissisticAlly wounDeD.

DeniAL is not A river in AFricA!

If and when I think of other things to admit, you'll be the second to know.

I'm also very gifted, a good friend, occasionally wise, irreverent, rather extravagant, curious, outspoken, opinionated, quite brave, very flexible, power·full, and live mostly in my sense of humor.

I am a seeker, a believer and a creative being. My furniture is all white.
I drink only red wine.
This makes me some kind of optimist.

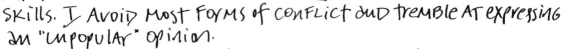

Also, I have a black cat.

it was my first real furniture and I still get nervous that I can't just pack up all my stuff in a car anymore. I'd have to get movers— does this make me grown-up?

I'm stubborn, trusting, sarcastic, and an introvert who's learned extrovert skills. I avoid most forms of conflict and tremble at expressing an "unpopular" opinion.

Once we've rambled through our dry and tame places, we can begin to explore succulence. Succulent Wild Woman is a process, and an adventure. To discover, and recover, your own succulence is a voyage of the interior and exterior. Succulence comes from your center— the sweet, true part of you—your essence— that belongs to no one else.

Wildness is relative. Wild is a state of mind that relates directly to succulence. We are each in a process of being and becoming a
    Succulent Wild Woman!

I am sharing my own journey so that you can be a part of my exploration.

I AM very reAL— Deeply HumAn, pArtly HumAn, splendidly and Horribly imperfect, Bent, Disguised, loud, ever-changing, thought·Full and thought-less, wildly nArcissistic in certain spots.

How Are you most HumAn? WHAT WOULD A MAP of you look like? THere Are so mAny wAys to Be nAmed and Defined, yet We Are Ultimately A Mystery. WHAT A Glorious thing!

I'M an Aries with VirGo rising and A Scorpio Moon, A 9 on the enneAgram, A SAGE in the MicHAEL teAcHings, A Secret and Skeptical Christian, A DABBLING BUDDHIST; and in A committed and monogAMOUS relationsHip with A Man.

We Are All complex, imperfect HumAn Beans.

little BeAns, Just BouncinG Along

I AM pArticulArly interested in WOMen, and lovers of WOMen. WHen I stArted writing this Book, I WAS worried thAt Men might Feel left out:

Then, I recAll HeAring MAYA angelou recite Her MAGnificent poeM, "PHenomenal WOMAn," AT HerBST TheAtre in SAn FrAncisco. SHe sAiD,

"Before I reAD this poem, I just need to sAy thAt I Know there Are A lot of incredible Men out there, and thAt this poem MAy seem to excLude them — it Doesn't. AND I want to sAy to All the Men out there, Honey— you Got to write your own poeMs!"

write your lives so thAT others MAY Be illumiNATED

How we stop ourselves

I am always "turning away from the ecstasy." There are things I know I love doing, yet I stop. Why?

Everytime I meditate, there is a benefit. Still, I stop myself all the time from doing it. My mind is filled with fresh and realistic reasons about "why it's not time to meditate." Exercise creates more oxygen and a "new mind," but I am almost frantic to postpone it. Eating well provides an almost instant reward. Yet I run to empty foods from childhood that used to comfort me, and now are sedating.

I'm often seduced by struggle.

It's as though it's painful to feel "too good." I'm used to the effort, and sometimes confused by the joy.

The structure of struggle was made up of junk and fear

I am familiar with rejecting pleasure, and with a low-grade, almost constant feeling of despair. There are many companions for this journey, even though it makes no sense, I find myself clinging to sadness to avoid feeling my emptiness, or even happiness!

sadness was slippery and kept changing shape it wasn't nourishing

She tried clinging to the sadness even though it repetitively hurt her

I think it is easy to stop ourselves from being too bright, too happy, too successful.

Conformity also soothes us. We can predict it, and there is the illusion of control.

Unfortunately, we also stop ourselves from being too visible, unusual, or vivid.

"I am not eccentric! It's just that I am more alive than most people. I am an unpopular electric eel in a pond of goldfish!"

DAME EDITH SITWELL

We stop ourselves from being too loud, too different, or too MUCH.

Yet we crave our individuality, our wild, special selves. We want to live our adventures and be seen for our essences.

Who are you after the guests have gone home? Who are you after you take your makeup and clothes off? What do you dream about? Who are you reading? How do you stop yourself? Who are you?

WAYS YOU STOP YOUR SELF:

Working with the Hard Parts

I am often running from pain

MY TRACKS COULD BE SEEN IN THE SNOW

When I feel helpless or out of control, I want to close up. Wall off. Medicate. The ego maniacally says No! to everything. I listen to it, and isolate to try to avoid the pain.

Pain Arrows Arrive silently and sometimes with no warning

SHE FOUND A CAVE WHERE SHE THOUGHT PAIN COULDN'T FIND HER

Even the idea of pain: possible pain, invented pain, perceived pain, imagined pain, future pain, and, especially, present pain.

If pain seeps in, I seal off the entrances with some kind of barrier: distraction, food, sleep, bad TV movies... yet pain continues to seep until it bursts in, in some unguarded entrance, and catches me sleeping at 5 A.M., and I awaken sobbing.

"When something within us is disowned, that which is disowned, wreaks havoc."
Ralph H. Blum & Susan Loughan, The Healing Runes

It is clear that breathing into the pain works with body massage. Perhaps it also works with emotional pain. Turning toward a large wave in the ocean is the best defense. Diving into the huge wave can save you.

We MUST work with the PARTS THAT HURT

IF THere is DARKness, We HAVE our FLASHLIGHTS. IF
there is terror, We HAVE our GOD. IF there is DespAir,
FeAr, anxiety, anger, or AGony, We can Become our
Own Best pAreut and HOLD the little CHILD inside of us.

Faith

THis
Tiny
CHILD
is WAITING
For comfort From you

When you WALK to the eDGe OF All the liGHT you Have
AND take that First step in to the darkness of the unKnown
you MUST Believe One OF twO thinGs Will Happen:

There will Be SOMETHING soliD For you to stand upon,
or, you will Be tauGHT HOW to FLY

Patrick Overton

From ReBuilding the Front Porch OF America © 1996

How can we Be open to the HArD pArts
and still Function? OH NO! not This
We SAY. WHATever This MiGHT Be:
an incApAcity, A weAkness, A CrueL
THOUGHT, A DeATH, A Misunderstanding,
A Joy not SHAreD, A wistFUL, lonely
MOMeut.

This MUst Be our GreATest TeAcHer.

note: reAD the poeM:"THe GuestHouse" By Rumi

I Myself still FiGHT with ALMost every This THAT
Comes My WAY.

Working with the HArD pArts and not AGainst
them will creAte Movement.

INVESTIGATING the DARKNESS
WITH A FLASHLIGHT

A woman called my inspiration phone line and said, "I feel inspired by you because you are still investigating your dark sides — this gives me hope."

I used to avoid the darkness, the shadows, as much as possible because I mortally feared what might be hidden in there.

Then I was propelled into the darkness by memories of incest, self-destructive behavior, and other traumas.

SHINE YOUR LIGHT INTO THE DARK SPOTS

My therapist speaks beautifully about the darkness in a poem he wrote called, "The Museum of the Lord of Shame." This is an excerpt from his forthcoming poetry collection.

CODA

When you are small there is no protection
from shame
& now that you are older
your attempts to keep the unsafe out
costs you more than you can imagine
We need to breathe in the direction of danger...
& to sing
We must not only be wounded
-- For surely all of us are that
But be willing to suffer
The terrifying healing,
with its stations of humiliation,
shame, endurance & grief
             -- GARY ROSENTHAL

THe GOOD news is THAT BloCKinG THe DARKness
Also BloCKs the Joy, and the succulence.

WHen we can FACe the DARK, we will Be FlooDeD By
the LiGHt.

Then we can Dance together in the Glowing

I keep BuilDinG BARRicADes, HiDinG FRom pain,
DistrActing Myself FRom AGony, and then I wrench Myself
out of My illusion of sAFety and FACe the WORK.

· WHAT WAKeS YOU AT 3 A.M. and Feels SCARy?
· WHAT is your DARKest FeAR?
· How Do you HiDe FRom DARK places?
· WHAT Does investiGAting the DARKness sound Like to you?

"WHen you FACe pain Directly sHe will Give you an ointment
so the wounds Dont Fester."
Ruth Gendler

IF we use A FlAsHLiGHt wHile investiGAting the DARKness,
we will HAVe A GuiDinG BeAcon. PerHAps We can sHine it
on neGlecteD pARts thAt neeD LiGHT or Be AwAre thAt
Many others Are in the DARKness, stumBlinG and exploring.

My therApist Also tAlKs A lot ABout HolDinG the
pArts of Myself thAt Are wounDeD or crippleD. I usuAlly
turn AwAy and resist. SometimeS I Do try, and
I crADle somethinG uGLy in Myself and WATCH it
soften and transform.

I HAVe seen terrifying sADness transform
with the crADLinG.

43

WOMEN'S HEARTS ARE BIG enough to BEAR the pain, peer into the DARK, and DO the work.

We Are led into DARKness anyway By events of Life: DEATH, loss, and pain. We cannot pretend that we Don't live with the DARKness, or smile it AWAy or think somehow we will escape.

There is no need to escape!

"The LIGHT AT the end of the tunnel is A Freight Train. ONLY GOD is Driving."
SARK

I will Be in the DARKness too! We Are not Alone and our HEALING touches everyone.

Our HEARTS Are reAlly very close together.
We Are All ACHING, seeking, BREATHING, crying and Hoping . . .

I send you the welcoming of the DARK

BLOCKS to Succulence

Being present in the Darkness by CHERI HUBER

THE Highly Sensitive Person BY Elaine Aron PH.D

eMBRACing your inner critic By HAL stone PH.D & SiDRA Winkelman stone PH.D

THE SPIRITUAL Of THE enneAgram Dimension By SANDRA Maitri

PROCRASTINATION BY Jane Burka PH.D & Lenora Yuen PH.D

STAND STILL Like the HUMMingBiRD By Henry Miller

WiSH CRAFT BY BARBARA SHer with Annie Gottlieb

You CAN HEAL YOUR LiFE BY LOUISE HAY

CHANGE your Handwriting! Change your Life By Vimala RoDgers

LivinG JUICY By SARK

WOULDN'T nothing FOR MY Journey Now By MAYA Angelou TAKE

LiFE DOESN'T FRIGHTEN ME POEM BY MAYA Angelou PAINTINGS BY Jean-Michel BASQUIAT

resources

- innerlinks.com/Angel-CARDs. Intuitive Solutions, "A set OF CARDS THAT HEIPS YOU think THROUGH DIFFICULTIES, MAKE DECISIONS in HARMONY WITH YOUR VALUES AND integrity, AND TAKE inspired AND effective ACTION." By CO-CREATORS JOY DrAke & KATHY Tyler

- BelonGinG: REMEMBERING OURSELVES HOME BY TOKO-PA Turner TO PURCHASE GARY ROSENTHAl'S 16-PAGE CHAPBOOK THE MuseuM OF THE LorD OF SHAME FOR $5, Plus $1 FOR POSTAGE, GO HERE: www.GARyrosenthal.net/THE-lorD-OF-SHAME

Feeling Safe as a Woman

I remember reading a book called <u>Places in the World a Woman Could Walk</u>. It was fiction, but the title really spoke to me about feeling safe. I feel unsafe a lot of the time, and when I walk alone (especially after dark), I know that luck and denial play a part in my carefully constructed "illusion of safety."

I was walking at the beach the other day with two friends, to watch the sunset. A woman approached us and told us that she felt nervous, that she thought someone was following her. She said,

"It was a black Chevy Blazer, and he went by me really slow about 5 times. So I went into the woods over there to hide, and men were saying really scary things to me there! So I ran out. Could I just walk with you?"

We drove her home, and I told her never to hesitate to ask for help — that if you have a "funny feeling," it usually means that something is going on.

Being stalked or followed by someone and feeling like prey is a horrible feeling. Sometimes, men don't understand it. Smaller or shorter men get a taste of it. It's a primitive thing, to feel like a target.

I pray for the safety of women all over this world

I'm glad that so many self-defense classes are being taught now. Especially the ones that use full impact against padded, trained instructors who actually assault you. The theory is to retrain our bodies to fight in perilous situations, by reprogramming what we've been taught, have lived with, or think.

I'm working up my courage to take one of these classes. I think they need to be taught in junior high and high school.

Another way to feel safe is to talk about feeling unsafe. If we use our voices to describe, explain, ask other people for help— this subject will be a part of our conversations and not secret or hidden like the crimes themselves are.

Ultimate safety lies in the acceptance of safety as an illusion. We can prepare, train, fight, defend, study, or carry a large weapon and none of it guarantees our safety.

I am cautious, fairly informed, use my intuition, avoid certain areas, always lock my car doors— and I still walk alone at night. We all bargain with what we can and can't accept living with.

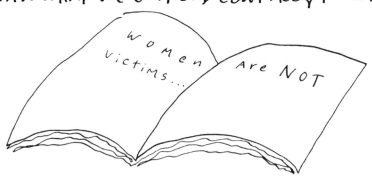

Beginning Ways You Can Fight Back

- Practice yelling "NO!" loudly from the bottom of your stomach. Many women are weak "no" sayers.

- Contact a self-defense class and ask if you can attend a graduation ceremony for a demonstration.

- Read about violence against women.

- Talk to other women and men about safety. The more that we collaborate with silence, the more that violence can grow.

- Be aware that in public places "being nice" has no place. If you get into an elevator and feel weird with another person, get out — with no thought of politeness. Almost every victim of attack has had a funny feeling right before violence occurred.

- Walk boldly and confidently. Project an aura of "Don't mess with me."

- Study how victims are developed and how you might be participating in a victim mentality.

- Pray and meditate for change.

I wish for all of us the lessening of violence against women and, eventually, the disappearance of this particular form of violence as we become trained, empowered, and society wakes up.

Going out Alone

I call them "captive women." They never go out without a man, or a group of women. If questioned about going out alone, they make squeamish faces and say,

"I couldn't go out _alone_. It wouldn't be any fun."

Even women who are not like this are shy about going out alone. There is still a social stigma about being out "alone" (translation: boring, desperate, nobody likes her). Going out alone is a skill and an art that can be learned, shared, and implemented.

When I go to restaurants alone and the host greets me with, "Just one?" I smile and say, "Oh — one is more than enough — you'd be surprised." Then I sometimes explain that simply saying "Table for one?" is more gracious and welcoming.

What you can bring along to assist you in being alone confidently:

TOOLS: Something to write in/on Something to read

Attitude: Confidence, Curiosity, Openness.

Don't worry if you don't feel any of these — just act "as if."

I go out alone to bars, restaurants, movies, events, on walks, and have traveled alone extensively.

If you learn and practice an attitude of confidence and take your own tools, you will begin to feel more free in the world, to go anywhere by yourself and create your own magic.

if you already know how to do this, please help other women learn it!

Practice saying this: I am welcome everywhere. A place is lucky to have me visit it.

Another useful skill is talking to strangers — striking up a conversation is an art to practice. Some of it involves mild eavesdropping, which we are taught not to do, and most of us do anyway. You simply find people that interest you, and find a spot to comment, ask a question, or deliver a compliment. Most people are receptive. If not, you'll feel it right away and can busily read or write something as a diversion.

I have also made fake phone calls from pay telephones to seem like I had a "purpose"

One time, I spoke to a man in a bar wearing a leg cast and a safari suit. He turned out to be the son of a famous author, who had been raised by living in hotel suites all over the world.

We drank very expensive old port and I listened to his travel stories for most of the afternoon — the stories and the man were fascinating.

We cannot meet or be met if we don't speak up, or take a chance. How can you deny someone the pleasure of meeting you?

The label looked like it had come from a pirate ship — torn & yellowed very authentic

let's all boldly talk to new people!

We Are not Alone in this world.

It just seems That Way sometimes.

My Friend, Robin, who recently turned 40, just told me That she's started going out Alone For the First time in Her Life, and That she loves it. "The Freedom to go Alone Happily to the movies is marvelous."

Take yourself out on A Date. Get All Dressed up and Go somewhere expensive. People will stare and wonder,

"Who is That Fascinating woman?"

I used to send so many customers to this elegant restaurant in the Bahamas That they set up A Table Just For me. I would come in with my sketchbook and sit Alone. I Always met people and Had conversations.

A sketch book is a Fine Dinner Companion

You Are Fabulous and interesting All By yourself

Besides, if more and more women go out All By themselves, we'll Begin to see each other, and can join each other's Tables!

I promise you this: if you Develop your Abilities in Going out Alone, you will Begin to Forget That you're out By yourself! It will Also Double your chances of meeting A romantic interest— if you're By yourself.

Traveling is another Dimension of Going out Alone. It Takes A kind of intrepid Faith.

Go! see the world! Take solitary walks and meet other kindred spirits.

Bring your walking stick and speak with the wood spirits

Being Self-entertaining

I call them "self-entertaining units" — women who can visit you and function well by themselves. I used to have houseguests that hovered near me with plaintive eyes and whining requests. "WHAT SHOULD I DO NOW?"

We can develop self-entertaining skills. Women are taught to cling and cluster and need to redevelop the ability to be self-entertaining and independent.

Attitude: · Keen interest in others and environment
· exploratory mode
· ability to collect stories along the way
· open eyes
· Fresh mind (everything is new)

Equipment: · Journal/sketchbook
· letter writing kit
· walking shoes
· books

Expand your self-entertaining equipment by including whatever you like that you can do alone, or share with others.

There is bravery and confidence involved in being self-entertaining, yet the more you develop these skills, the more others will want to be with you!

We can all think of fascinating women who are always off exploring something — the world provides for these women by opening doors to brand new experiences.

This way to a brand new experience

One of the reasons we depend upon others for entertainment is because we don't trust ourselves to provide it.

When was the last time:

- You deliberately got lost in your car?
- Called a brand new person?
- Went on an exploring walk with no destination?
- Took yourself out for an exquisite dinner?
- Planned a solitary trip/retreat?
- Had a serendipitous adventure?
- Went by yourself to a movie?

Being self-entertaining is a gift you give to yourself and others.

The gift is you!

Now my houseguests bring me stories and presents from their adventures out in the world!

Heart shaped rocks

A bright leaf

ripe fruit

Wood that drifted

Smooth and friendly peobles

Entertain yourself well— you will be surprised at what a good guest you are.

Remember: the real luxury is in your interior.

FEAR of BEING "too MUCH"

All my Life, I've HEARD THAT I'M "too MUCH." Too wild, Too loud, too outrageous, too emotional, too sensitive, Too needy,

TOO MUCH

My boyfriend and I HAVE both Been called "larger than life." When I met Him, I asked Him if He felt "larger than life." He put His Hands on my shoulders and looked into my eyes:

"Susan This is the size Life is. Anyone who tries to make you smaller is just A Lilliputian."

I knew Then that I HAD found the right man For me. If we Don't Fully use who we Are, then who Are we?

As I Age, I see the temptation To Laugh A Bit less loudly, Ask less, "tone Down" For the benefit of "others." Often I Don't even know who these "others" Are, But They might be upset, so I comply.

I was Actually warned in A restaurant one time For Laughing too loudly!

The Manager came over and said crabbily,

"Some of my customers Are annoyed by your Laughter— Why Don't you keep it Down?"

I Asked who these customers were. He refused to say, so I stood up and said,

"Could I see A show of Hands of people that Are upset By the sound of my Laughter?"

I WAS not Laughing very loudly.

No one raised their hands, so I said to the manager, "Good. The matter is settled."

So, let's risk wearing something that's a bit "too much," laughing "too much," and loving "too much."

Write and tell me if you've ever been told you're too much, and we'll start a society:

THE TOO MUCH SOCIETY

We'll have too much parades!

Certainly, we'll wear hats that are too much, and eat too much chocolate

and then we'll take too many naps!

OLD, Alone, and Succulent

I met my friend's mother. She is in her 70's and very feisty. We had a tea party, she and I and her son, and when they were leaving, I told her she was a succulent wild woman.

"How?" she asked, her eyes flashing. Her son looked nervous. This fueled my answer.

"By the way you flung your head back while lying on my chaise lounge, by the way you tried on my painted silk cape with such flair and style." *she has lots of flair and style*

Her son was blushing, and his mother said, "I'll have you know that I danced alone the other morning — the jitterbug! I haven't forgotten at all."

If we marry our fears — being old and being alone — we come up with the terrifying phrase, "old and alone." Yet, why is it so terrifying?

We're all getting older everyday. One day, we will be old women. We can be fabulous old women, or crabby, unwilling old women. It's our choice.

let's all be fabulous old women!

Sometimes age brings health challenges. We can meet these challenges with love or resistance, allowing or rejecting. Of course, it isn't always easy.

We are studying now to be the old women we will be. Take the right courses, give yourself tests. We can welcome any alone-ness and magnify the goodness in it. Celebrate the great parts of being alone.

Our Fears turn "Old and Alone" into a nightmare. We must live in our dreams and know that old and alone is nothing to fear.

We will be succulent wild old women!

"The problem comes when we want to cling to a particular thought or idea. The mind always wants to cling. I'm 60 years old, and if I'm still clinging to being 40, then I'm in trouble."

RAM DASS

My mother is facing living alone at age 73 after the death of her husband and the end of their 46-year marriage. She dearly misses him, and their life together.

She has also begun to see some blessings.

The other day she called to tell me she was planning her new bathroom in her new home, and said,

"Pink towels! I'm going to finally have pink towels. I've always wanted them, but didn't think it was fair to your dad to have such a feminine bathroom."

THICK
THIRSTY
Perfectly
Pink
Towels

We all have our versions of pink towels!

Fears

Dancing in The Flames By Marion Woodman

Love letting is Go of Fear By Gerald Jampolsky

The Fear Book By Cheri Huber

The Crone By Barbara G. Walker

Awakening the Warrior Within By Dawn Callan

The Language of Emotions By Karla McLaren

Women who run with the wolves By Clarissa Pinkola Estes PH.D

How to Do the Work: By Nicole LaPeria

Recognize Your Patterns, Heal From Your Past, and Create Your Self

Persephone returns By Tanya Wilkinson

Two or Three Things I know For Sure By Dorothy Allison

Playing with The Heart Chess wood By Beatrice photos by Marlene Wallace

Warrior Marks By Alice Walker

All I Did Was Listen By Rachel Awes

resources
- RAINN, The Rape, Abuse And Incest National Network, A Multilingual, 24-hour counseling And Support hotline, 800-656-HOPE, www.rAinn.orG
- National Domestic Violence Hotline, A crisis intervention support for victims And their Families And friends. Multilingual, 24 hours, 800-799-SAFE, www.thehotline.orG
- Big Fat Lies Women Tell Themselves: Ditch Your Inner Critic And Wake Up Your Inner Superstar By Amy Ahlers

Movie
- Inside out

Importance of Being Crabby

Could we all just admit when we're crabby? My mother used to answer the phone in a FAKE cheerful voice,

"Hellloooo!" right after yelling at us.

So often, we "put on a HAPPY FACE," "grin and bear it," "smile — it can't be that BAD." Sometimes it can be!

Being crabby is real and it's healing. It can help us get closer to what's wrong, or what hurts.

answering the phone was more important than how you felt

If you say to a friend, "I'm just crabby right now," they can usually tell anyhow, and sometimes it opens up a dialogue. If you say to other women, "Are you crabby?" they usually love it.

I like doing this on the phone with service providers who sound crabby. If you say something, it gives them permission to be human, and can result in a fabulous, honest exchange.

Crabbiness dissolves with the right kind of attention. Of course, there is also overcrabbiness, rampant crabbiness, or what my mother calls "the crabby Appletons" (people who are crabby for a living and want to stay that way).

Remember to be crabby consciously! Women are great at being crabby and can do much more celebrating about it.

CRABBY and PROUD

FLY A CRABBY FLAG!

Self Healing

We all have the ability to self-heal. Whatever we've done, we can be forgiven. In our essences, we are truly innocent.

What does essence look like? A glowing, spinning orb?

I'm a survivor of sibling incest, physical abuse, rape, and am "almost an alcoholic." I've taken most "recreational" drugs and been on welfare. I've attempted suicide. I've binged on food and explored my codependency. I'm moderately neurotic and am currently examining my narcissistic structure. I have tendencies to be depressed, worry, and see things negatively.

I've been rebirthed, psychologically evaluated, in therapy, massaged, chakras cleared, psychically healed, had acupuncture for emotional reasons, read many, many self-help books, attended workshops, classes, talks about the inner child, the dysfunctional family, AA meetings, OA meetings, Alanon meetings, met with healers, listened to channelers, had out-of-body experiences, studied A Course in Miracles, been hypnotized and floated in sensory deprivation tanks. There's more, but this list is making me tired!

Currently, I'm in individual therapy and group therapy. I still read self-help books, but not as compulsively. I practice meditation and mostly love my life.

I pray a lot.

Every time I meditate, there is resistance. Usually, I can welcome it. Sometimes not.

60

I HAVE pretty HEALTHY ADULT FriENDS, AND AM in love with AND loving A MAN WHO is BECOMING MY PARTNER AND BEST FRIEND.

I'M DOING WORK THAT I love AND LIVING MANY of MY DREAMS.

I AM Continuing To self-HEAL THE WOUNDS AND HOLES left over FROM EARLIER LIFE. I cry MORE, FEEL DEEPER, AND HAVE MORE TOOLS To NAVIGATE through TOUGH TIMES with.

SOME HOLES ARE LARGER THAN OTHERS... SOME ARE CAVERNS...

"I'M no longer AFRAID of STORMS, FOR I AM learning HOW To SAIL MY OWN SHIP."
                    LOUISA MAY ALCOTT

explore HEALING options. If you FEEL UNLOVED, LOOK To yourself for love. WHATEVER THE issues ARE, ULTIMATELY self-love AND ACCEPTANCE ARE THE ANSWERS.

We ALL HAVE tiny, MIS-SHAPEN PARTS of ourselves THAT we HIDE AWAY AND DON'T love. TURN TOWARDS THOSE PARTS AND CRADLE THEM.

I KNOW AND BELIEVE STRONGLY THAT WE ARE EACH OUR OWN BEST HEALERS. SometimeS we NEED GUIDANCE or other people To ACTIVATE OUR self-HEALING.

Give yourself THE GIFTS of self-HEALING.

 Your presence is THE ACTUAL GIFT.

THERAPY

WOMEN ARE receptive to therapy, I think, BECAUSE of their Attention to the emotional Aspects and need To Be HEARD. I'M Always AMAZED when women Don't Try, or HAVEn't trieD, therapy. WHo else will listen so raptly to you?

IDEALLY WE WOULD All BE ASSIGNED Some KinD of Spiritual ADvisor AT Birth. WE COULD turn to this person All through our lives For perspective, GuiDance, and Free ADvice. Some of us AlreaDy HAVE this in A PArent or GrandParent. THe rest of us COULD HAVE an "internal GrandMother."

THere is still A STIGMA ABOUT "Going to therapy," As THOUGH THere is something wrong with you, or it is self-inDulGent to pAY someone to HELP you with psychological work. YET WE PAY our CAR Mechanics, our Gynecologists, or GARDeners. THis is curious. WHAT is More important than our psychological HEALth?

I WATCH WOMEN repeating patterns, Acting unconsciously, or lost in Depression and wonder why they Don't seek HELP. Often WOMEN will sAy, "I Don't know any GOOD therapists."

HELPING HAND

SOMETIMES WE ARE STUCK IN A MAZE of our own MAKING and COULD USE A HELPING HAND

Perhaps not, but other women do. Ask them. Therapy can be the acceleration out of a stagnant pattern, the support needed for an important change, the guidance for rebuilding self-esteem.

STAGnant pattern

She rode away from stagnation

Friends can also provide some of these things, but it's not their profession. A dedicated therapist's _only_ professional purpose is your psychological health.

A large percentage of women have been sexually or physically abused~ some of these women have never received any kind of therapy. I was one of these women. It took a failed suicide attempt and a brave friend asking, "Why aren't you in therapy?" (Thank you, Lisa!)

We can be those brave friends for each other.

A Tribe of Brave Friends

When I started therapy, it was terrifying to sit in a small room with a woman I didn't know, feeling exposed and

Telling Her my secrets.

Now I've Been in therapy For 8 years, Both individual and Group work. I continue to Go not Because I have problems, But Because it enriches me, and I AM Growing. I'm Also FASCiNATED By psychological process work.

We contain so MUCH AS WOMEN. We Are so complex, stuffed Full of Feelings, Memories, HALF-Truths, Denials, Hopes, and yearnings.

We Deserve to Be Fully Alive psychologically!

Celebrate your own PSYCHOLOGY!

explore your own interior

SHAre WHAT you Find in THere

read words From your soul

Y O U   Are VALUABLE

JUST AS You Are

remember: HeALinG is an inside JOB

HEALING PLACES

We heal from the inside, in certain outside locations. Here are some of my favorites:

Ocean: Waves remind us that there are reliable patterns like our breath. Also, the negative ions in the air actually change brain waves.

Woods: We are surrounded by tree families and sheltered by their canopies. Keep hugging trees.

rocks: We are reminded that growth and change can be microscopic and result in something solid.

Waterfalls: Falling water speaks of constancy and power.

Gardens: In the gardens, our hands touch the growing things and our hearts fill.

Tops of Hills: Overlooking the world, we see tiny cars or towns and gain perspective.

We Also Heal in inside locations. Here Are some of my reliable spots:

BATHTUB: FLOATING in WARM WATER, surrounded on All sides, TEARS can FLOW out of us and join the WATER everywHere.

Beds: SoFt and Thick, SAFe places to Hibernate and DreaM.

Forts: tiny nooks of privacy and escape. reMeMBer the SAFety of A GOOD Fort?

PHones: psychic sound CHAMBers, one on one, intiMate conversations Can TAke place Without Distraction.

Groups: in certain KinDs of Groups, THere can Be profound SAFety and exploration in the company of others.

Planes: Speeding through the sky in A Metal CAPSule eMPHASizes the iMPortance of Trust and release of control.

Closets: in the BACK of the Closet is A tiny Door. THrough there lies narnia · · ·

In our Hearts is wHere the HeALinG occurs. We can TAKe WHAT we experience in the outside, and Bring it in For HeALinG.

WoMen's HeArts Are rAre, Deep and wide. we Do Contain MULtituDes!

I send you rADicAL self-Acceptance, power.FULL HeALinG, and the MirACle of your HeArt SPeAKinG — and you listeninG.

A room of your own

Women need space to be creative. Creativity thrives in solitude. It can be a tiny space.

When I was 10 years old, my grandfather had a little house built for me and delivered on a flatbed trailer. It had electricity, sliding glass windows, and a dutch door. I immediately "moved in" and began cooking creative projects. It was my sacred creative spot.

Now I'm 42 and live in the "magic cottage." It's a 180-square-foot former tool shed, and not much bigger than the playhouse of my childhood. I have bells on the door that I put out when visitors are welcome. When the bells aren't out, nobody can knock. This gives me privacy and solitude for creativity.

Women live such accessible and intimate lives — we are often physically or psychically open to other people. It is even more important, then, to have "rooms of our own."

Special thanks to Virginia Woolf, who wrote about a room of one's own.

My friend Kathryn was living in an apartment with her husband and very young son, and craved a space in which to create. She put up a tent in the corner of the apartment, and stuffed it full of her jewelry supplies, doll making materials, and other creative treasures.

A fort full of creativity

We all have odd, unused spaces that could be turned into creative retreat spots.

Creativity suffers under close scrutiny—ours or someone else's.

We all need a space of our very own that is like the soup pot— Always simmering and getting better with age. WHAT's in your soup pot?

Give yourself space to lay out paper, leave paints in a scatter, a few beads on a scrap of velvet, a bit of wood that blew in from the sea.

I love you

Nourish your eye and spirit with inspiring things. They will bloom with your tending.

Things to try for Healing

There are so many tools and resources for healing available to us as women. Begin to keep your own "Healing Book" of things you have tried, or would like to try— then, share your list!

THE HEALING BOOK

Sometimes just reading the list feels healing to me

Here is a list from my Healing Book:

long solitary hike
comet watching
moon bathing
telephone support
Breaking things
letters never sent
rituals, Burnings
Motherpeace Tarot
Giant Bubble Bath
poem writing
collage making
Meditation
crying
Journaling

WHAT feels healing to you?

Hot springs
i ching
rune stones
Acupuncture
SAGe, incense, candles
throwing things AWAY
inner CHILD CARDS
transformation GAMe
angel CARDS
BACH Flower remedies
DrUMMInG
Sweat lodges, saunas, Hot tubs
HeALing places
reading Healing words
HiDing
complaining to someone with no solutions offered
LAUGHing until your STOMACH Hurts
listening to AUDio tapes
HeALing videos
visiting an inspiring person
telepathically communicating with an animal
Being of service
Going to A Movie in DAytime, By yourself
prayer
More tears
We Are not Alone in our HeALing work!

MORE FROM the HeALING BOOK

How to Forgive Your Father

I AM not DADDY's little GiRL.
I'm A MOUNTAIN lion in A SKIRT, With
PRAYERS in MY HEART.

When I ASKED MY DAD WHAT He wanted
in A "DREAM DAUGHTER," He SAID,
"I wanted A DAUGHTER WHO WOULD WEAR an
APRON and MAKE SOUP FROM A HAM Bone."
I'M A VEGETARIAN WHO DoeSN'T COOK.
My "FANTASY FATHER" WOULD Be super literary
and WORK AT HOME.

My DAD WAS A TRAVELING SALESMAN WHO
Struggled With spelling.

When I WAS 4, MY DAD'S HEAD WAS AS BiG
AS The WORLD! I rode on His SHOULDERS,
CLASPING His ForeHEAD with MY tiny HANDS and
LAUGHING AS we ran Through The GRASS.

TOGether We Were tAller than GOD.
My DAD HELD My red SCHWINN BiKE AS I BALANCED
My First solo trip, and ran ALONGSIDE Before letting
Me Go to peDAL into A new WORLD.
My DAD Always Got MAD AT Dinner and I Thought it
WAS Because of Me So I SAT up straight and tried to Do
it All perfect and He still yelled. His DAD Got MAD AT Dinner too.
I Finally learned that when I COULD SHOW SOFTNESS, MY DAD COULD
Show support. I WISH I'D HAD More time To Be With HIM. I remember
WHISKER rubs and "serious TALKS" and standing on His Feet to Dance Around
the Kitchen. He tied My ice skates DOUBLE-TIGHT, and There WAS ALWAYS Love—
LARGE and raw and imperfect. When I prowl Through All the prayers in My
HEART, and in certain photographs in A special KIND of LIGHT, I can
see My DAD'S FACE inside My own, SAYING, "STICK WITH Me, KID!"
I KNOW now THAT He loves Me in His language — that The PAST stuff is just
FOG on the Mirror— that The little GIRL inside never stopped loving HIM.
SHe Feels the love and Forgives the pain.

Hey DAD! I'll love you Forever, you know.

in Memory of Arthur JAMES KENNEDY ♥

©SARK 97

HEALING

Beginning to Heal By Ellen Bass & Laura Davis

Second Firsts: A Step-by-Step Guide to Life After Loss By Christina Rasmussen

Healing into Life and Death By Stephen Levine

The Inner Child Workbook By Cathryn Taylor

on Death and Dying By Elisabeth Kübler-Ross

It's OK that You're Not OK: Meeting Grief and Loss in a Culture that Doesn't Understand By Megan Devine

No Enemies Within By Dawna Markova Ph.D.

I Know Why the Caged Bird Sings By Maya Angelou

A God Who Looks Like Me By Patricia Reilly

Anatomy of the Spirit By Caroline Myss Ph.D.

The Courage to Heal By Ellen Bass & Laura Davis

I recommend the movie Harold and Maude.

resources

- Voice Dialogue and the Psychology of Selves tape series. By Halstone, Ph.D and Sidra Winkelman Stone Ph.D, www.voicedialogue.tv
- Sounds True catalog recordings, learning tapes for the inner life, www.soundstrue.com
- Eden Method: Empowering You with Energy Tools for A Life You Desire edenmethod.com
- On Being onbeing.org
  The On Being Project is a nonprofit media and public life initiative. Includes a public radio show, podcasts, new ways to experience poetry, and tools for the art of living.
- IFS Institute ifs-institute.com
  Internal Family Systems is a transformative, evidence-based psychotherapy that helps people heal by accessing and loving their protective and wounded inner parts.

MUSIC

- The Memory of Trees By Enya
- Neroli By Brian Eno

Adventuring without Money

I wish for women to explore the world and open as many doors as possible. There are many ways to have adventures with little or no money, and lots of creative thinking.

There are many doorways to adventure

During my twenties, comfort meant very little so I traveled with tiny amounts of money and lived day to day. Islands were most intriguing to me, so I found ways to visit and live on them.

I slept on chaise lounges by the pool, taught swimming lessons, baby-sat, house-sat, or accepted hotel rooms from managers who admired my spirit.

I spent a lot of time on Paradise Island, in the Bahamas. The turquoise water is translucent blue and the sand is shocking white, or the color of chocolate chip cookie dough. There are bright green casuarina pine trees and sudden giant clouds.

Casuarina pines are soft and feathery

There are statues of strong women with moss in their armpits and lizards in their hair. Things are slightly unkempt and crumbling in the islands. Secrets abound.

Wild cats come out to eat the scraps of food from fancy restaurants. The men and women are golden and laugh easily.

One of the costs of adventuring is that you are faced with yourself. You cannot escape by going to a job and doing lots of activities. Having little money promotes contemplation.

Sometimes what you find inside of yourself is not easy to look at.

Mostly I ate mangoes naked, went barefoot through the hibiscus petals, slept helplessly for countless hours, pinned to my bed by transformative dreams. I also felt desperately lonely in paradise, and like my life had become a humid tropical failure.

One of my favorite ways to adventure was to keep moving — so I went to explore Jamaica.

Jamaica is a wonderland for succulence, and for women. In the islands, people are ripe. Like the fruit.

I spent a number of beatific months living in Ocho Rios, Jamaica. I called everyone I knew and told them I was staying forever.

Jamaica was the closest thing I'd ever seen to the movie, Swiss Family Robinson and my dream of living in a treehouse.

I met a man named Bongo Silly who lived in a treehouse, and rented rooms in the branches — he had dozens of pairs of Keds tennis shoes, in all different colors,

and cooked unbearably delicious soup.

I sat at a table made from a door, my bare feet on clay earth, and ate soup out of a seashell with a hand-carved wooden spoon.

I also met a man who lived beneath a waterfall in a cave that had glittering walls. His name was Fuck-up, and his specialty was grilling vegetables that he grew himself. To get to his cave, you had to wade across a river and climb on smooth stones warmed by the sun.

The smooth stones warmed by the sun

Both of these men were not "educated" in the ordinary sense, and I learned that spirituality often lives in simplicity.

There were many mysteries in Jamaica, and I went eagerly from one to another, tasting all that I found.

I thrived in the barefoot, outdoor living that I found in the islands — wearing bright bits of cloth and being in the sea. I learned a lot about my physical self in these places.

There was a freedom in the way of life that opened me

Another outrageous adventure I always wanted to experience was living in New York City. When I was in my early twenties, and still living in Minneapolis, I became intrigued by the subject of obscene phone calls. I began collecting research for a book by interviewing the <u>callers</u>.

Nobody had ever done this. I placed ads in newspapers across the United States that read, "If you make obscene phone calls, call me."

The results were fascinating, and I asked my best friend at the time to join me in my trip to New York.

We rode our bicycles from Minnesota to new york with the accumulated research. When we arrived in new york city, I called the _new york post_ and told them to send a writer and photographer (the pictures turned out to be too revealing to print in the paper).

Then I called the _washington post_ and told the story to columnist Maxine Cheshire. She did her whole column on the story of the "book," front page.

This got us into Doubleday to meet with their senior editor. We sold the book idea by telling stories. He arranged for us to stay in various empty penthouse apartments while we tried to write "the book."

working title: CALLS of the WILD

Instead, we partied with millionaires, appeared on radio and tv, and talked all the time about "the book." It was exhausting, and we weren't writing anything. Then our friendship developed problems while trying to collaborate.

We finally turned in a proposal after Doubleday threatened to cut off access to our penthouses (this had gone on for a year!).

Doubleday responded:

"This is the _worst book proposal we have ever seen in all of our years of publishing_ — but, we want to see anything else you write because there is a certain energy."

I didn't even hear the second part. It was my worst fear come true. I wasn't really a writer,

I'd FAILED, I'd never publish, and There was no Hope for Me.

I Left New York soon After That, and Moved BACK to Minneapolis, and Moved into The little playhouse My Grandfather HAD Built For Me. [Mice From Mars]

I'd written My First Book in this playhouse AT AGE 10, and Thought I'd try writing everyday and see if I WAS Really A writer.

It WAS Desperate and Difficult and I Don't know How I Managed to Continue—But I DID. The worst Thing WAS That My writing Bored Me!

During My Thirties, My Adventures were More in My own interior As I lived the Life of A "STArving ARTiST" Trying To Find Her creative place in the world.

I Believe it is important To continue HAving outrageous Adventures All Through Our Lives—in WHATever Forms they Take.

Women can explore The world even More By Bravely Traveling Alone, Being willing to work Along The WAY, Arrange for Fair Trades and BArters, rely on other Women and Friends, write About Their experiences, SHAre their stories, and en-Courage other Women To Have More Outrageous Adventures!

My Most Outrageous Adventure right now, AT AGE 42, is learning to love and Live intimately With another Human Being. I'll keep you posted.

Traveling Alone

All GOD's CHILDren need Traveling shoes

MAYA Angelou

I envision A world Filled with women traveling Alone, and meeting each other on the path...

I love traveling Alone for these reasons:

- The sense of ADventure is very clear
- All my tastes and preferences Are Honored
- meeting "strangers"
- sipping tea for hours
- no Destinations but my own
        the sense that anything could Happen

The challenging parts to traveling Alone Are:

- Being scared
- Feeling All Alone
- relying only on yourself
- not meeting anyone

PACK A BAG with tiny treasures and Favorite clothes that cheer you

Then I realized that I feel All these things when I'm Home! Where have you Always wanted to Go? Plan A mystery Trip To places you've Always wondered About (the mystery part is mostly you.)

ONE TIME, I WAS TRAVELING WITH A MAN I HAD MET in MONTE CARLO, and WE WERE HEADED to PARIS. SUDDENLY, I KNEW THAT I HAD to experience PARIS BY MYSELF. I ASKED if HE WOULD MIND SPLITTING UP and MEETING AGAIN lAter. He FELT offended By this request and STALKED off the train.

As the train pulled out of the station For PARIS, I FELT NEARLY UNBEARABLE excitement AT the iDEA of ME and PARIS MEETING.

SHAKESPEARE and COMPANY

I went on to Live in A BookStore—ABOVE the SHELVES, BEHIND A purple velvet curtain, and ACROSS From NOTRE DAME CATHEDRAL. I worked in the Bookstore in exchange For rent.

I KNOW THAT if I'D still Been with My FrienD, this ADVENTURE WOULD not HAVE HAPPENED.

I HAD TO STEP into MY own sTORY...

I HAVE often FELT CALLED to Journey BY MYSELF—and I'm not PARTICULARLY BRAVE either. In FACT, I Get HOMESICK very EASILY, and SOMETIMES JUST HIDE in My tent All DAY. EATING CHEESE and CHOColate For "COMPANY."

SWISS CHEESE
DARK CHOCOLATE

Yet, so Many ADVENTURES SPEAK to us WHEN We TRAVEL Alone. It's AS though the ADVENTURE TAKES the place of A person.

STRETCH your trAVELING Alone Muscle. STArt with tiny Trips, or leAp into the glorious UNKNOWN of A BiG Trip.

WHere HAVE you Always wanteD To Go?

Don't WAiT! TrAVEL Alone...

Adventures Close to Home

Women deserve Adventurous lives. As little girls, we served Flower petals on plates made of leaves, and imaginary liquid in thimbles, wearing skirts made of old tablecloths.

The table might be an old tire

We Adventured on our bicycles, which turned into imaginary horses. There were daily adventures, close to home, beneath the clothesline, in homemade forts, and in our best friends' bedrooms.

As Adult women, we can become more sedate, less experimental— we develop "Adventure Amnesia" and don't even remember what is lost.

Then we're invited to a tea party and feel a fizz of excitement.

come to A tea party with remarkable women. Wear a hat.

Or, we take a "Miracle Walk" in our neighborhood— Just to look at trees.

WE GO OUT DANCING TOGETHER AND WEAR WILD NAIL POLISH... (M AND D, THIS IS YOU!)

We REMEMBER OUR ADVENTUROUS SOULS. I LIKE TO TAKE MY SLEEPING BAG AND DRIVE TO THE COUNTRY DURING COMET ACTIVE TIMES. I HIKE TO A HILLY SPOT AND WATCH SHOOTING STARS.

FULL MOON HIKING IS ANOTHER GRAND ADVENTURE. EXTENDING OUR ANTENNAE CAN PRODUCE ADVENTURES IN "ORDINARY PLACES."

While WALKING ON A CLIFFSIDE TRAIL WITH MY FRIEND, DEBBIE, AROUND THE BEND APPEARED A MAN IN AN ELEGANT SUIT AND TIE — AS THOUGH HE HAD JUST WALKED OUT OF A MAGAZINE. I COMPLIMENTED HIS APPEARANCE LOUDLY AND HEARTILY, AND HE GRINNED AND INTRODUCED US TO HIS 2 JAPANESE FRIENDS, ALSO WEARING SUITS. THEY DISAPPEARED DOWN THE PATH, AND WE LAUGHED AT THE INCONGRUITY OF IT.

A TINY ADVENTUROUS MOMENT, CLOSE TO HOME. IT CHANGES YOUR PERSPECTIVE, REMINDS YOU THAT THE WORLD IS DEEP AND RICH AND FULL OF COLORS AND MIRACLES.

Fill your Life with tiny and LARGE ADVENTUROUS MOMENTS.

Perfect peaches, lilting street Musicians, A Butterfly landing on your shoulder, Happy Dogs on the Beach, people praying together outside, Children wearing pajamas in the daytime, old women on benches, laughing.

These are all signs of Adventure.

We must be open to Adventure — seek it out, ask questions, dare to talk to strangers.

Women are oppressed by fears in this society. It's true. It's not safe. Neither is staying home, hiding from an adventurous life.

Take self-defense, use your intuition and caution, walk in pairs and groups, but please, come out of your houses, apartments, and cars.

Your Adventures Await you!

OUTRAGEOUS ADVENTURES

TRACKS BY ROBYN DAVIDSON

Don't PUSH the river BY BARRY STEVENS

THE WONDERFUL FLIGHT TO THE MUSHROOM PLANET BY ELEANOR CAMERON

I SHOULD HAVE STAYED HOME edited BY ROGER RAPOPORT and MARGUERITA CASTANERA

GUTSY TRAVEL TIPS and WISDOM FOR THE ROAD WOMEN BY MARYBETH BOND

THE AIR CONDITIONED NIGHTMARE BY HENRY MILLER

SARK'S JOURNAL and PLAY! BOOK BY SARK

MAIDEN VOYAGES: writings of women travelers edited BY MARY MORRIS in COLLABORATION with JACCY O'CONNOR

A FOXY WOMAN'S GUIDE TO TRAVELING ALONE OLD BY JAY C. BEN-LESSER

WITHOUT GUIDE- contemporary women's TRAVEL ADVENTURES edited BY KATHERINE GOVIER

Travelers' TALES: A WOMAN'S WORLD BY MARYBETH BOND

THE SIZE OF THE WORLD BY JEFF GREENWALD

THE independent WOMAN'S GUIDE TO EUROPE BY LINDA WHITE

resources

- The transformation game, blessing cards, intuitive solutions and angel cards. All wonder-full resources to inspire you! To order: Innerlinks Associates, Joy Drake and Kathy Tyler, co-creators, address: PO Box 10502, Asheville, NC 28806, website: www.innerlinks.com
- Moonlight Chronicles: a wonder-full handwritten exploration of waking and looking at life. "Why Are We Here?" "Where Is Here?" PO Box 109, Joseph, OR 97846, www.moonlightchronicles.com
- Henry Miller Library, Highway 1, Big Sur, CA 93920, 408-667-2574, "Serendipity in a Redwood Grove by the Sea," henrymiller.org
- Eat, Pray, Love by Elizabeth Gilbert

MUSIC
- New Beginnings by Tracy Chapman

Movie
- Auntie Mame

Succulent Shy Women

I've had many varied sexual experiences, and I'm still shy sexually.

I want to honor myself and any other woman for being shy about expressing herself sexually, or describing what she needs or wants.

Succulence does not always mean wild abandon or juicy freedom—sometimes it is a quiet unfolding, a peeling back to reveal a tender center.

I know I've felt pressure to be sexually wild, free—like a warrior Aphrodite! Sometimes I've acted out others' fantasies and not my own.

Right now I'm exploring a softer, more vulnerable sexual me.

There is a shy part of me that wants long, quiet explorations with my sexual partner. Where you press your faces close together and share deep secret wishes before being sexual and where you can say,

"Slower please. Slower still."

Sometimes sexuality can seem so explicit or graphic—it can be scary. I'm allowing shyness to be present, to include it in my succulence.

Succulent shy woman

let's welcome our quiet parts.

Succulent Shy Woman Waking Up

If you would like to explore your sexuality in less shy ways, here are a few suggestions:

Read erotic literature written by women. There are wonderfull poems and stories that can privately and quietly inspire you.

Watch videos or television programs that explore sexuality.

Draw a sexual map of your body in your journal: Describe your body sexually in great detail, as though you were creating an "owner's manual" for someone else to read. Consider sharing with a lover.

Let your sexual self write a letter: your sexuality has things to share with you that you may not be able to hear in ordinary circumstances. Start your letter: "What I need or want sexually."

Invite a lover to take a body tour of you. Light candles, blindfold him/her, and set a 15-minute timer. Explore only for this time. Switch if you feel like it.

Keep a sexual journal with your lover (or invent a lover). Write passages about what you want, or what you liked.

He smelled faintly of vanilla, and wore a soft shirt, after our bath together. We lit candles and

Gently explore yourself sexually. Open new territories.

erotic robots

I've been an erotic robot. My definition is: using the body sexually without soul. Being an erotic robot also occurred when I would try to satisfy lovers in bed by doing things that satisfied only their fantasies— not my own. I felt like a performer, and would "leave my body" in order to function sexually.

When I look back at my times of being an erotic robot, I see a young woman plunging unknowingly into worlds of others' imaginations.

I was afraid to really know myself sexually, or be truly intimate with a partner. I am still afraid.

So many of my episodes sexually took place because I couldn't say no and wanted to be adored.

I sometimes made love just to "be polite" or to get it over with so the other person would go home! (maybe if he comes, he'll go).

Once, I was seduced by advertisements for "erotic dancing." "perfect for artists and students, no touching permitted, let out your wild self!"

Perfect job for terrified, lost souls, who also need money

I was 22 years old, and for $20 an hour, it seemed perfect.

I couldn't figure out how to put on my g-string before dancing. Once on stage, I moved woodenly and like I was underwater. I remember a lot of men in plaid shirts yelling things at me. There was a lot of sadness and shame in the room.

It was awful and I quit that night.

There were other times I attempted to have a "sex positive" experience by dancing or modeling erotically. They all failed.

I like the idea of taking the shame out of it, of women dancing erotically in a positive way. Until our culture fully embraces women, I'm not sure that it's possible to make that realm positive. Perhaps the women who are trying to change this will succeed—I hope so.

My experiences were shaming and soul-less. It taught me that my body is precious and not separate from my soul.

I thought I could make a lot of money fast, be outrageous and show off my dancing and body.

The fantasies and words of these men were not honoring or even fun. It felt desperate and very, very sad.

The erotic robot was a frozen performer

I've retired the erotic robot part of myself now. She stands mechanically in my memory as a reminder of how, as women, we are soft and irreplaceable and very human and alive—especially sexually.

I honor my times as an erotic robot and do not regret them (although I wouldn't mind erasing certain things).

Now there are much more fascinating things to learn and explore about myself sexually.

As women, we deserve to be erotically alive, exploring our sexual mysteries and yearnings.

My Sexual Mysteries

Vibrators

"Home is where I plug in my vibrator."

SARK

I got my first vibrator at age 21. It scared me, so I kept it in a shoe box in my dresser for quite awhile.

On Easter Sunday, I was supposed to visit my parents, and didn't really feel like facing the day, so I took out my vibrator.

I used a towel to cushion my skin from the machine (secretly I was afraid of being electrocuted), and proceeded to experiment.

Very quickly, and with fantastic shock waves, I experienced the most powerful, glorious orgasm I had ever had!

WHY HADN'T SOMEONE TOLD ME ABOUT THIS?

I felt quite startled and puzzled by the intensity, and after briefly recovering spent a lot of that afternoon practicing. Later, I bounded down the stairs of my house shouting,

"Happy, Happy Easter!!"

I continued practicing so much in the week after Easter that I became pale and rather exhausted. I finally shared my vibrator experiences with a girlfriend and confessed to having 50-60 orgasms in a day! I've always been an extremist.

She pointed out that I might be overdoing it —
just a bit. HA!

And so, I am a committed vibrator user. I
wish I'd had one when I was younger. I think it
would have meant less AWKWARD sex in the bushes
with my first boy friend. and more orgasms for me!
The bushes were an "instant bedroom"

note: vibrators are no better than, or capable of
replacing, lovers. Have no Fear!

Boys are "TAUGHT" and even encouraged to masturbate.
Girls are not.

I was given a pink booklet about menstruation
and warned about pregnancy. nobody talked about
pleasure — especially self-pleasure!
Your Menstrual cycle

Why are we not taught and encouraged
to pleasure ourselves as women?

I know women who have never had an orgasm.
Then there are countries/cultures that perform genital
mutilation and remove the clitoris so there can
be no pleasure. read WARRIOR MARKS by Alice Walker

The more we learn about our own bodies and
orgasms, the more empowered we'll be to share
sexual pleasures with a partner, and with ourselves.

WOMEN DESERVE SEXUAL PLEASURE!

Vibrators Are GOOD

Brave Wonderings

I wish for women: the freedom to sexually explore without shame. The ability to be conscious sexually. The awareness of self-pleasure, and knowledge of their sexual bodies and discovery of their "sexual spirituality."

I wonder if I have been so damaged by incest that I cannot be healthy sexually. I wonder if the years of unconscious self-destructive sex really taught me anything?

I wonder if I will ever feel truly at home in my body and at peace as a sexual creature.

I wonder if I will write openly about being bi-sexual, and if people will be intrigued, repulsed or horrified. I wonder if I will be horrified, repulsed or intrigued. Why don't I feel free to just be bi-sexual?

I wonder why we don't talk more about masturbation, the dark side of sex, and why women are often such sexual victims.

I wonder about shame and sex and how they're connected.

I wish for women:
The release of sexual victimization and the courage to stop violence and objectification of women. The creation of a sexually postive world where we can have open dialogues about our sexual wishes, hopes, fears, and dreams. The wisdom to speak openly with our children about sexuality — the facts and the mysteries, and everything in between. The gift of safety in sexuality. Sexual peace of mind.

90

Sexual Mis·steps

I first titled this "Sexual mistakes" but then I realized that I don't believe in mistakes as much as Mis·steps, stumblings.

Creative exploration will always result in mistakes, and if we fear those, we risk paralysis and a numb, "good girl" mentality.

Our morality may guide us in our sexual exploration. Is your morality yours, or the regurgitation of parents' and/or religious beliefs?

What are your sexual beliefs?

Do you believe:

· Women can be sexual only in marriage and/or relationship?
· Women can explore sexually by instinct?
· Heterosexuality is better than homosexuality or bisexuality? Different? How? Why?
· Sexuality should/not be openly discussed?
· Sexual health and happiness is a right or a privilege?
· Sexuality is natural and healthy?
· Sexual expression needs to be encouraged/repressed?

Write down your sexual beliefs. Question yourself. You have the right to explore yourself sexually.

I would like to see young women write sexual "mission statements" that could guide them in their discoveries sooner.

My initial beliefs about my sexuality were shaped by rebellion, pain, instant gratification, and naiveté.

What would your sexual mission statement include?

If we spend more time shaping our beliefs, and honoring those beliefs, our steps could become more sure on our sexual paths.

I think that all my mis-steps led me to uncover my sexual beliefs rather late in life (and I'm still uncovering!). As I stumbled, I grew.

I had no role models of vibrant, passionate, outspoken sexual women.

In high school I became known as a "slut" because I spoke openly about sex. I played strip poker, so I was a "bad girl" (usually I won and made the boys take their clothes off!).

I wish I'd gotten therapy sooner to help me in exploring myself sexually.

I wish I could have told the truth sooner to all the lovers I was performing for. I wish I could have forgiven myself along the way for my mis-steps.

I wish that I'd learned a little earlier about shame and how to manage it.

In honor of the mis-steps, let's, as women, take responsibility for ourselves sexually, and emerge as positive, sexually alive role models. Perhaps I can be a role model too.

I send you the courage to make your own mis-steps and keep walking bravely forward.

"And remember, we all stumble, every one of us. That's why it's a comfort to go hand in hand."
                                    Emily Kimbrough

Sexually Blossoming

My sexual past will no longer determine my sexual present.

I will learn to speak gently and specifically about my sexual needs and desires.

I will tell the truth faster sexually.

I will continue growing sexually and not stagnate out of fear or lack of knowledge.

I will take my sexual temperature often, and report findings to myself and to my partner.

I will learn more ways to be sexually intimate.

I wish for you an opening, a loosening of old judgments or fears, a sexual lightness and well being, sexual curiosity, and abundance.

May we open to the sun and let light into any dark places. May we allow the dark and learn from it. May we laugh during sex play and be sexually awake.

"You can clutch the past so tightly to your chest that it leaves your arms too full to embrace the present."
Jan Glidewell

What is it about sex? I'm afraid to admit my mistakes, my failings. The soft vulnerable spots that I'm polka-dotted with. I fear being too graphic. I fear scaring people. I fear scaring myself. I know so little sexually. How dare I write about it? Do I deserve to be sexually safe and happy? Why not? How can I inspire sexual bravery in myself and others?

Let's open our sexual closets and gently investigate and share the contents.

SEXUALITY

Allies in Healing by Laura Davis

Awakening your Sexuality by Stephanie Covington Ph.D.

The Sexual Healing Journey by Wendy Maltz

Women, Sex and Desire by Elizabeth Davis

The Couple's Comfort Book by Jennifer Louden

Soulful Sex by Dr. Victoria Lee

150 Most Asked Questions About Midlife Sex, Love and Intimacy by Ruth S. Jacobowitz

The Good Vibrations Guide to Sex by Cathy Winks and Anne Semans

Sex for One by Betty Dodson Ph.D.

resources

- The Good Vibrations Store: Fun place to order a vibrator
  1210 Valencia, SF CA 94110, 415-974-8980, Mail-order catalog: 800-289-8423,
  www.goodvibes.com
- Sex and Love Addicts Anonymous
  PO Box 1964, Boston, MA 02105, 617-625-7961, slaafws.org

Marrying Yourself

My boyfriend used to ask his mother,
"How can I find the right woman for me?" and she would answer,

"Don't worry about finding the right woman—concentrate on becoming the right man."

We must become the women that we are first, before entering fully into a relationship (some women can do this work while in a good relationship).

So often, I just molded myself into whatever the relationship seemed to need or require.

One time, after a long-term relationship had ended, a friend challenged me and said,

"Can you just spend some time Alone now?" *I never really had!*

The idea of being alone terrified me. So I got a cat. This helped.

Buddha said: "if you want to learn about love, start with plants and animals—they're easier."

I entered a long period of celibacy, therapy, and learning to fall in love with myself.

Learning to fall in love with yourself is an immense challenge—I'm still learning!

I began to have conversations with other women about being alone, and what it meant to us.

I MET TWO WONDER·FULL WOMEN AT A PARTY

We SPOKE of "CELIBATE DATING," of MEN FRIENDS, AND MYSTERIES of ROMANCE, of CLAIMING OUR OWN TIME, of SCULPTING, JEWELRY DESIGN, AND of the WONDER of BEING HAPPILY ALONE, AND HOW COUPLES ARE SOMETIMES HELD UP AS the IDEAL· I SAID,

"PEOPLE DON'T TALK ABOUT HOW MUCH WORK it is to BE A COUPLE!" ONE of the WOMEN SAID,

"WHEN you're ALONE, you can CREATE your OWN MYTHOLOGY AND NOBODY CHALLENGES you. IN A RELATIONSHIP, your OWN BULLSHIT GETS REFLECTED BACK MUCH QUICKER."

I FOUND THAT SOCIETY is MYSTIFIED BY WOMEN ALONE. WE DON'T COMMONLY CELEBRATE ALONE·NESS the WAY WE CELEBRATE COUPLES· NOBODY SAYS,

"HOW'S your LOVE life? WITH yourself?'

FOR AWHILE, I NOTICED COUPLES EVERYWHERE. EVERYONE SEEMED to BE "in love" EXCEPT ME. THEN I BEGAN to REALIZE the GIFTS THAT learning to love MYSELF GAVE.

<u>FINALLY I WASN'T WAITING to BE LOVED</u>!

I took VACATIONS ALONE, BOUGHT CLOTHES FOR MY TASTES ONLY, READ BOOKS UNDISTURBED, AND TURNED off the PHONE FOR DAYS AT A TIME. THE SILENT PHONE

Then, it seemed time to be in union with myself, so I performed a metaphorical marriage, and promised to love and honor myself until the end.

What this meant was that instead of waiting to be married or partnered, I decided to marry myself in a ceremony by the ocean with a private ritual to celebrate.

Try this: Marry your self. Create a small wedding in nature, or somewhere special to you. Invent your own vows or promises, buy yourself a ring and flowers. Love and honor yourself until the end of time!

I had truly stopped looking for a partner, and wrote in my journal how at peace I was, but if I was looking, this is the type of lover I would want:

A Bundantly creative.
Deeply Generous.
Funny.
Doesn't snore.
Embraces emotions.
Wonder. Full

A truly creative and eccentric person to spend ordinary and remarkable moments with.
lover

want your soulmate to have

Try this: Make a list of what qualities you would

Then I also felt it was time to stop therapy, and began the process of termination. I said, "The only thing that could keep me in therapy would be if I fell in love."

The following week I met Craig.   p.s. He snores.

FACES of INTIMACY

NOBODY tells us AS little GIRls thAt we MAY FALL in love and HAVE MOMents of HATING our BeLoved, or HAVE ridiculous ArGuMents AT 2 AM. over SOMething neither person understands.

My Friend JOHN cALLs it, "the nuance of annoyance." After you've Been with someone for Awhile, ALL the tiny and lARGe things they Do thAT annoy you, COme ForwArD.

We Are not TAuGHT something I CAll "intiMate neGotiAtions." It involves ADjustMent, COMProMise, integrity, Truthtelling, options, willingness, and HeArt·Full listening.

I WATCH Friends WHo I ADMire in this AreA, and there is A softness, an inclusiveness in the WAy they speAK.

Their GOAL is union.

I either isolate Myself, or Try to "TAKE over" with loud suggestions, DetAiLed Directions, and rigid ideAs. My GOAL is frequently BEING RIGHT.

My BoyFriend sometimes cAlls Me "substitute TeAcher nancy," WHich is our signAL thAT I've Gone too FAR, or AM MARCHING to some non·neGotiAble Drummer. (of cOurse, He sometimes AppeArs As A substitute teacher too!)

We often stART over.

As I learn and nAviGate these intimate wAys, THere is A panic, or A KinD of terror thAT sometimes Arises: AM I DoinG it riGHT? BeinG FAir? MeetinG My neeDs? MeetinG someone else's neeDs? expressinG Myself, Yet maintaining AppropriAte eMotiOnAL BOunDAries?

"Intimacy happens in moments. The mistake we make is in wanting it all the time."

JO ANN MAGDOFF

Actor Sharon Stone said, "Give me a thousand men in the audience, and me on the stage and I know exactly what to do. Give me just one man and me on a couch together, and I'm really scared."

Emotional storms pass through me frequently and since I generally try to resist most feelings as soon as I feel them, they tend to get stuck, be projected, or hoarded for attack later.

I envy the people I know who seem to communicate less out of their heads and more from their hearts (I'm working on allowing this!).

The "faces of intimacy" are all around us. They are infinitely more human than I ever thought.

Women deserve rich, emotional, intimate lives. We also need to understand ourselves intimately before we can recognize all the "faces of intimacy" and the many forms it takes.

I know that I'm in a process of letting go of romantic expectations and embracing new, tender, intimate moments that appear in ways I never imagined.

THE "GOOD GIRLFRIEND" MUST DIE

As I advanced in my love relationship, I began to notice an insidious part of my personality that seemed to arise often. I named her, "the GOOD Girlfriend," and this is what I wrote about her:

The "GOOD Girlfriend" always knows what to bring to a potluck, makes good potato salad, does all the communication tasks, makes her hair big and sexy, compromises about where to sit in the movies, is available, isn't "too serious," is sexy, doesn't say FUCK, is available, blends with her partner, is assertive but fake, wears a pretty MASK, is a "nice Girl," shares feelings—but not too many!, seems spontaneous, but isn't, is angry, but says she's "annoyed," is full of rage, but says she's "upset," controls her feelings in a suitable container, doesn't change plans at the last minute, listens attentively, but is actually not present, looks sexy, yet doesn't live in her body, seems power-full but is actually power-less, doesn't dwell on unpleasant topics, buys the gifts, carefully controls atmosphere and environment, makes sure things are "pleasant," gives up when conflict feels thick, reveals only her best and finest qualities, does not FART audibly, definitely does not FART exuberantly, holds most feelings in and smiles through a tight and suffocating MASK, always has effortless and pleasing orgasms.

the end!

I HAD ABSORBED YEARS of CONDITIONING ABOUT HOW I THOUGHT WOMEN NEEDED TO BE SO THAT SOMEONE WOULD love them.

One DAY, MY BOYFRIEND and I HAD BEEN invited to A BARBEQUE, and the "GOOD GIRLFRIEND" PART of ME BECAME terrified AT the THOUGHT of MAKING potato SALAD and WEARING SOMETHING "cute," SO I HID OUT and pretended to BE SICK. CRAIG FOUND ME in the BATHTUB and ASKED,

"Are you REALLY SICK? or DID you JUST not WANT to GO to THE BARBEQUE?"

I BURST into TEARS and SAID, "I can't BE your GIRLFRIEND! I Don't even KNOW HOW to MAKE potATO SALAD..." I BABBLED on ABOUT All MY FAULTS and HOW I DIDN'T FEEL "QUALIFIED" to BE loveD.

CRAIG HELD MY HAND, leaned over and SAID,

"you Don't understand. I'm CAPTAIN ODD! We Are perfect for EACH other. I Don't even Like potato SALAD! I Don't CARE if you ever MAKE it. I like you JUST AS you AlreaDy Are."

I HAD connected love and performance together. Love is A Mystery and Doesn't Keep Score. We Are worthy of love AS WOMEN JUST AS we Are.

"Our LIMITATIONS, our imperfections, our MISTAKES... These Do not reflect Our Inferiority, But Are PART of BEING HUMAN."

JOAN SHEINGOLD DITZION

101

Lessons in Love

"The First Duty of love is to listen."

PAUL TillicH

I Feel Like I've MADE lots of MistAkes and learned lots of lessons in love. From My First BoyFriend AT 16 until now AT 42, I Figure I HAVE 26 years of inexperience.

1970 1971 1972 1973 1974 1975 1976 1977 1978

and then we JUMP to... 1996 and BeyonD...
1997

I USED to seek out MArrieD Men so that they wouldn't expect too MUCH From Me. It wasn't until MUCH lAter that I realized that I DiDn't think I DEServeD A "real relationship."

COMMitment problems were something I continually BlAmeD on Men— MUCH later I Discovered that I WAS terrified of COMMitment, and CovereD this up By continually choosing "BAD" men who weren't AvAilAble.

Sorry, not AvAilAble

EMBRACing eACH OTHer HAL Stone & SiDrA WinkelMan

There Are so Many excellent Books now and people working to unravel problems and provide cLArity in the realm of love relationships.

Still, it takes truth-telling and consistent practice. I HAD A Friend who SAiD She would Always choose to HAve some therapy in A relationship. She SAiD,

"I'll never be in another unsupervised relationship again."

She and her partner had started therapy, and it was a tribute to the supervision of a guide, a healing companion for our psychological selves.

I'm amazed that anyone gets along! When you think of idiosyncracies, unconscious projections, restimulations from the past, and the relationship history of your partner, it's stunning that <u>love</u> <u>works</u>.

My history involves: married men, violent men, liars, con artists, the immature, the "not ready," the lost, the desperate, and the users.

* I've also been most of these myself at different points.

Women are often the adaptors. They mold and change to fit a relationship. We need to question our needs and desires, and ask questions like:

· What does support feel/look like to me?
· What is a conscious relationship, and am I in one?
· is my partner committed to communicating and working with emotional stuff?
· Does my partner want to be in a relationship?
· Do I?

Women also are initiators. Let's initiate growing, healthy, fun love relationships.

"Love keeps no record of wrongs."

Apostle Paul

record
Book
of
wrongs

Living the Process

I HAD A Friend WHO TALKED ABOUT "real love stories" WHICH is the stuff you Don't HEAR ABOUT DURING The romance pHASE.

It's WHERE you Go on A long trip and He splashes GASOLine on your SHoe and WHistles too loudly.

It's WHERE SHe never wants to HEAR WHistling and complains THAT your SHoes Are squeAKING on THE GAS peDAL.

It's FinDing out WHAT lies BeneATH The FigHTS and SKirMisHes of DAily living. WHAT Are you really FigHTing ABOUT?

It's Figuring out A mutual language, Developing trust, increAsing intimAcy, telling The truth microscopically, and revealing yourself Deeply.

It's ABOUt Being exposed As wHo you really Are.

WHO is tHAt?

It is Being inDepenDent, interDepenDent, and Dependent.

It's ABOUt BuilDing A Best Friend· SHip with your lover.

Your SHip can Be WHimsical and SAil swiftly

love

It's about asking for what you need or want, regardless of the outcome.

I often see women settle for less because they're afraid of loss, lonely, needy, or having great sex.

The process of love is messy, holy, ordinary, and wildly hope-full.

Your heart will be very involved

Tell your loved one:

- What you truly feel
- Who you really are
- What you really want
- How to love you best
- How to listen to you

As women, we deserve to be fully met, deeply loved, and equally at play in the process of loving.

love calls on parts of you that cannot speak

"Love as a power can go anywhere. It isn't sentimental. It doesn't have to be pretty, yet it doesn't deny pain."

SHARON SALZBERG

MOTHERHOOD

In childhood, we play dolls, simulate births, and pretend to be mommies. Then we gradually find out that we can actually <u>be</u> mommies.

When I was 11, my mother told my brother and I that she was expecting — on April Fool's Day. She was 41 and it didn't seem likely, so we laughed.

My brother, Andrew, was born in September 1965 and I was the happiest big sister ever. I got to practice being a mom and I loved it.

I still tell people that I used to change his diaper, and at 31 years old he answers, "Not recently."

I terminated 3 pregnancies in my 20's because I felt there was no other way. I wish I had been ready. It is one of my greatest dreams and biggest fears to become a mother. I think it is the bravest human act to become a parent.

I watch my friend Adrienne, who soars as a mother. She is more open, allowing, and full of love than before. She turned to me in the delivery room after giving birth and said,

"Susan, this is <u>Big Love</u>."

Zoe
Arielle
is gorgeous

Zoe is my godchild, and I marvel at her perfection. She is a teacher for me. Motherhood is a sacred trust, a holy act, and a trip of surrender.

Whenever we give birth, adopt, or act as temporary mothers, we have this maternal gift, this nurturing ability, and it is divine.

We Are All mothers in special ways. Godmothers, Big sisters, Aunts, or simply Friends with Children. There Are so many Children Already Here who need love — it isn't necessary to Be A Mother to experience Mothering.

Children Are our teachers and Healers

"Women without children Are Also the Best of mothers, often, with the patience, interest and saving grace that the constant relationship with children cannot Always sustain. I come to crave our talk and our children Gain precious Aunts. Women who Are not mothering their own children Have the clarity and focus to see deeply into the character of children webbed By Family. A child is fortunate who feels witnessed As A person outside relationships with parents, By another Adult."

Louise erdrich, The Blue Jay's Dance

© 1995 By Louise erdrich and Harper Collins publishers Inc.

"Having A child is like Growing another Heart."

Rosie O'Donnell

Hopes

THROUGH All the relationships, we keep Hoping We'll Be Fully Met By someone FABulous.

"Hope is the thing with FEAthers that perches in the soul, and sings the tunes without words and never stops AT All."

Emily Dickinson

Hope keeps us answering personal ADS, Going on Blind DATES, meeting our Friends' Friends, or being set up By relatives. WHAT is she/he Like?

Even when we Are SATisFiED, and HAppily Alone, we entertain Hopes once in Awhile During romantic movies, or Holidays, or when we're sick. Hoping For A MArvelous union is not wrong. Hope is A GreAt Companion and Motivator. Even when I HAD stopped looking For A partner, A tiny part of Me still Hoped...

When Friends, Roy and VanessA SAiD, "He's the MAle version of you." I resisteD.

He couldn't Be All that they SAiD. Could He?
He WAS.

SARK's Journal and Play! Book

We Met AT A pArty For My third Book, on OCT 23, 1993. I WAS weAring A short BlAck Dress and Glowing neon eye on My chest. The initial Feeling Between us WAS so strong that we Acted very unchAracteristicAlly and Avoided eAch other For the rest of the pArty, and didn't TALK For 4 Months After that.

He lived in Los Angeles, and I HAD vowed to never Again Go out with someone who DiDn't live in the sAme city.

I SAW HIM AGAIN AT A BRUNCH IN HIS HONOR. HE WAS WEARING A PURPLE JACKET, SMILING, AND I HAD THE SAME STRONG FEELING AS THE FIRST TIME WE MET. AT BRUNCH, I PLAYED A GAME BY ASKING EVERYONE AT THE TABLE IF THEY SLEEP NEAT OR MESSY. I ASKED, "WHAT DOES YOUR BED LOOK LIKE WHEN YOU GET OUT OF IT?"

HE SAID, "NEITHER NEAT NOR MESSY. YOU JUST KNOW THAT A DANCE HAS TAKEN PLACE."

THERE WAS BUTCHER PAPER AND CRAYONS AT OUR TABLE, AND HE BEGAN DRAWING A PORTRAIT ON HIS PLACEMAT. I LOOKED OVER AND NOTICED THAT HE WAS USING ALL THE COLORS THAT I NEVER TOUCH — THE GOLDS, BROWNS, OLIVE GREENS.

THEN I THOUGHT SUDDENLY, "THIS IS THE MAN I'M GOING TO MARRY."

I HAD NEVER THOUGHT I'D MARRY ANYONE AND USED TO LAUGH AT PEOPLE WHO "SUDDENLY KNEW" ABOUT MARRIAGE. STUPID ROMANTIC IDIOTS.

THEN I REALIZED THAT HIS COLORS COMPLEMENTED MINE. I primarily use primary colors.

WE MADE ARRANGEMENTS TO HAVE TEA THE NEXT DAY. A FEW HOURS BEFORE, I ASKED MY ASSISTANT TO CANCEL. I FELT SO SKEPTICAL AND TERRIFIED. I THOUGHT, "THIS ISN'T EVEN A DATE. HE LIVES IN LOS ANGELES. HIS NAME IS CRAIG. WHY BOTHER."

HE HAD ALREADY CHECKED OUT OF HIS HOTEL AND SO IT WASN'T POSSIBLE TO CANCEL!

THEN HE SENT A FAX.

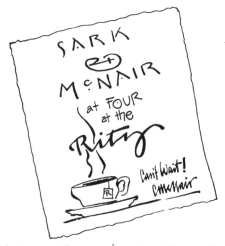

When I saw it, I knew I needed to meet him. Suddenly I became 13 years old, and couldn't decide what to wear. I tried on about 16 outfits before rushing off to the Ritz, 1/2 hour early, so I could get the best table.

When I arrived, He was already sitting there, waiting for the best table!

Within 2 hours, we were discussing our marriage, crying together, and laughing at each other's stories.

When I voiced my strong concerns about his living in Los Angeles, he said,

"Susan, real love moves."

This touched me deeply until I realized that he might expect me to move to Los Angeles! He said, "Susan, I will move to San Francisco."

So, in August 1996, He sold His House and is moving to San Francisco! (He moved. He's here now.)

and the love and learning continues...

I like to introduce Him as "the man of my dreams — and my nightmares."

I couldn't have hoped for someone so wonderful, or that I was this wonderful.

Love inspires Hope.

I am awed by Hope.

Love and Romance

Down in the Garden BY anne Geddes

I will never leave you BY HUGH; GAYle Prather

Operating instructions BY anne Lamott

Two part invention BY Madeleine L'engle

Succulent Wild Love BY SARK AND Dr. John Waddell

Embracing our selves BY HAl stone, PH.D; sidra winkelman stone PH.D

Secrets of A very Good Marriage BY Sherry suib cohen

Embracing the Beloved BY stephen and ondrea Levine

Conscious Loving BY Gay Hendricks PH.D and Katlyn Hendricks PH.D

Getting the love you want BY Harville Hendrix

The Jay's BY Louise erdrich

Blue Dance

The women's comfort book By Jennifer Louden

Soul mates BY Thomas Moore

Music
- John Coltrane Ballads
- Paul Cardall New Life

Movie
- enchanted April

Terror of Cellulite

Here's WHAT I've Done to try and eradicate cellulite:

- ridden A Bicycle 3,000 Miles
  (and I still HAD cellulite AT the end of it!)
- endured A 2-year cellulite MASSAGE program
  (intensely painful, very expensive.)
- ran 14 Miles A week compulsively
  (I Also Ate so little that I nearly Fell Asleep while running.)
- Tried CreAMS, LOOFAH SCruBS, steam HeAt and "wraps".
  (these worked For ABout 6 Hours.)

still, Cellulite creeps BACK. WOULD it Bother Me if I couldn't see it? Why is it so unsightly, and why Do I care?

PerHAPS I see it As A FLAW, or evidence of pain, or Being out of control, not in SHAPe.

Women can Be relentlessly Focused on Matters of Appearance.

I remember My First siGHTing of cellulite. I WAS A college FreshMan and HAD spent the First year eATing Donuts. I WAS trying on BAthing suits, and CAUGHT A rear view in the CHanGiNG rooM Mirror...

so Many Donuts

THe Horror of cellulite!

I've spent inordinate AMounts of time Arranging My thigh FAT while lying Down in the sun, so that no cellulite SHows, or BACKinG AWAy From A lover so He Doesn't see the BACKs of My legs.

SO MUCH HIDING

NOW I EAT CHOCOLATE, DRINK RED WINE, AND MAKE FEEBLE ATTEMPTS TO ACCEPT MY CELLULITE. FAILING THAT, I'D JUST LIKE TO SIT IN A LAWN CHAIR IN A PAIR OF SHORTS WITHOUT ADJUSTING MY THIGHS SO THERE ARE NO FAT BULGES.

MADNESS! I SEE THESE OBSESSIVE THOUGHTS AND MARVEL AT MY MIND'S ABILITY TO TRY AND MAKE IT "NORMAL."

MY FRIEND HAD A NEW LOVER, AND BEGAN BACKING OUT OF THE ROOM AFTER SEX, AND ALL OF A SUDDEN STOPPED AND SAID INTENSELY, "THESE ARE MY THIGHS. I HAVE CELLULITE. TAKE IT OR LEAVE IT."

HER LOVER REPLIED, "WHAT'S CELLULITE?"

LET'S LAUGH AT CELLULITE! START A CELLULITE ACCEPTANCE CLUB. FIND WAYS TO MAKE FRIENDS WITH IT. I REALIZE THAT CELLULITE HAS STUCK BY ME ALL THESE YEARS—IT MUST HAVE SOMETHING TO OFFER.

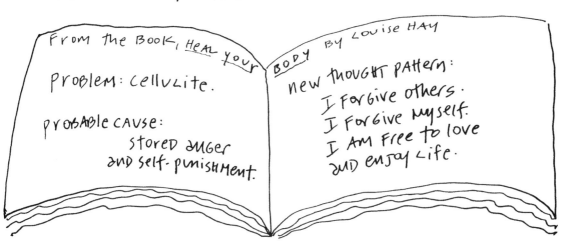

FROM THE BOOK, HEAL YOUR BODY BY LOUISE HAY

PROBLEM: CELLULITE.

PROBABLE CAUSE:
    STORED ANGER
    AND SELF-PUNISHMENT.

NEW THOUGHT PATTERN:
    I FORGIVE OTHERS.
    I FORGIVE MYSELF.
    I AM FREE TO LOVE
    AND ENJOY LIFE.

I ALSO THINK THAT IF WE COULD GET CELLULITE PUT ONTO BARBIE DOLLS, IT WOULD HELP A LOT WITH SELF-ACCEPTANCE.

Tyranny of Size

I remember being described as a "Big Girl" as a teenager, and to me, this meant FAT. One time, I was rejected by a dance teacher who told me I was "too heavy" to take ballet.

Perhaps He was terrified of loud, Actual-sized women.

Women are tyrannized by size. Sizes of clothes can haunt you. I wear everything from size 8-16. When I find something that fits me in a size 16, I feel like a huge tank. I have cut size tags out of clothes.

Size of body parts is also an ever-present awareness. For instance, I have small feet, which for women is considered dainty, feminine, and somehow pleasing. My friend Susan had size 9 feet at 12 years old and was told her feet were the size of boats.

She walked with her toes curled trying to disguise this. Big hair is considered good. Big legs, bad. Big bottom: worst of all.

I used to slam my hip against a wall to try and make it smaller. I started weight training mostly to make my butt smaller.

One time I was walking up the stairs in front of a lover, and he said, "You really do have a big butt!" I was devastated.

Sometimes I feel that my body is turning into a couch. Padded arms, big plump cushions, and even tiny uncomfortable pillows along the backside.

I continue to eat like an angry child—as if in a food trance—I repeat what made me sick the night before.

I feel horrified by the expansion of my flesh, ashamed that it matters to me so much, and defiant that I do not feel comfortable in my body.

So often I am paralyzed inside my body and barely notice its boundaries and edges. During sex, or trying to zip up a too-small skirt, or in a bathing suit, I become acutely aware of my physical self.

I am drawn to dance, to swing on the trapeze, to swim and run. I notice that I hide from these activities if I am feeling "too heavy" which is often a complete distortion of my actual size. There are also times I fall silent, my body critic numbed into some kind of peace treaty.   the white flag

Somehow as women, we connect our various sizes to our self-worth. We have mental images of ideal sizes—even if it's not in our heritage to be that way.

We know that men appreciate actual-sized women—and that other women struggle with this issue—yet we wish we could be smaller.

We want to shrink ourselves

We compliment weight loss, monitor our appetites, and shrink ourselves to fit some kind of standard. I wish we could all be the size we actually are. One size doesn't fit all—because there are as many sizes as there are women.

Let's look closer at the size of our hearts, the width of our souls, and the length of our spirits.

let your heart grow in size

"Phenomenal Woman" by Maya Angelou

Pretty women wonder where my secret lies.
I'm not cute or built to suit a fashion model's size
But when I start to tell them,
They think I'm telling lies.
I say,
It's in the reach of my arms,
The span of my hips,
The stride of my step,
The curl of my lips.
I'm a woman
Phenomenally.
Phenomenal woman,
That's me.

This is an excerpt from her fabulous poem. Read all of Maya Angelou's poetry.

Importance of Breasts

"LARGE BREASTS ARE like pets. Everyone likes THEM, but you're the one WHO HAS to tAKe care of them."   SARK

I HAD lArGe BreAsts AT AGe 12. nobody explained WHere they CAMe From, and I longed For the DAYS WHen I played BAsKetBAll with the GUYS, without A Shirt.

I Quickly learned to MAnipulate Men with MY BreAsts. (Also Known As Honkers, Hooters, BAzooms, HeADLiGHts, tits, BooBies, and Just plain BiG tits). I wore tiny tube tops, HAlter tops, too-SMAll t-shirts, and sucked in MY Stomach so MY BreAsts would look even lArger. I learned thAT Men stared AT MY CHest When we tAlked. I BeGan sAyinG, "stop stArinG AT MY BreAsts. MY eyes Are up Here."

I DiD the "pencil test" WHere if A pencil stAys under your BreAst, you HAve BiG BreAsts. I could weAr 2 pencils All DAY.

WoMen with SMAller BreAsts seemed so lucky to Me. I DreAMed of running without A sHelf of Flesh MovinG up and Down.

everything I reAD promoted either the sexuAl or MAternAl nAture of BreAsts

In MY scHool, Girls with BiG BreAsts were AutoMAtic sluts.

117

I saw my grandmother without a blouse one time. She had had breast cancer and was very matter of fact about showing me her chest. There was a long tight scar and I remember envying what seemed like freedom to me.

I grew bored with men's preoccupation with breasts, even though I still relied on their "power."

During my 30's, I began worrying about sagging breasts, and began wearing oversize shirts to try and hide from any scrutiny. I also developed posture problems from slumping down in an attempt to make my chest look smaller.

What is this obsession with cleavage?

I can appreciate the little tunnel made where breasts are pushed together, but it gets sweaty. You can keep things in there— money, perfume, or a phone number, and it's great for softening the butter at fancy restaurants. Men get delirious at the sight of cleavage (some women too). I think they imagine living in there. Just curling up between the breasts like giant soft pillows. Pillows with nipples.

"I used to be good at limbo until I grew breasts."
            SARK

I dream of a time where women stand proud and tall — whatever their breast size. Where breasts are not objectified, but just welcomed and healthy. Where all of us are satisfied with our breasts and their size.

RADICAL SELF-ACCEPTANCE

Someone called my inspiration phone line and left this message:

"SARK, I send you waking naps, where for brief periods of time, you can stop working on yourself, and simply luxwriate in where you are right now, just as you are."

I felt my shoulders come down about a foot and breathed deeply. All of a sudden, I saw this

incessant pattern of working and pushing

My boyfriend says he feels like sometimes we work on our relationship more than we actually just live in it.

Women are often immersed in renovation—of deep psychological explorations, long processing talks, relationship work, the heaving around of emotional boulders.

ABANDONMENT · Hyper-sensitivity · neediness

Whenever I hear the term self-acceptance, I usually think, "yeah, after I lose that weight, improve the cellulite, trim those thighs, meditate more often, be more fun to be with."

I propose a new way.

RADICAL SELF-ACCEPTANCE

Do not stand naked in front of your mirror and accept what you see.

Wear large pajamas and stay in bed all day and night.

BUY or BORROW self-improvement BOOKS, BUT DON'T READ them. STACK them Around your BEDROOM and Use them As places to rest BOWLS of cookies.

WATCH exercise shows on television, BUT DON'T DO the exercises. Practice Believing that the BENEFIT lies in imagining yourself DOING the exercises.

Don't power WALK. SAunter slowly in the sun, eATInG CHocolAte, And CARRY A BlanKet so you can TAKE A nAp.

SOFT nAp BlanKet

Stop looking At cellulite. ONLY view your BODY From the angles that Don't show it.

never vse A scAle. If your clothes Keep Fitting, you weigh the sAme. (Although it DoesN't reAlly Fit into rADiCAL self-Acceptance, I Feel COMPELLED to ADD A CAUTIONARY note From elizABeth TAYLor—"BewAre of elAstic WAisteD pAnts! you can Get quite FAT without reAlizing it.") THis HAS HAppened to Me.

Simply luxuriAte in where you Are right now. reAD this. Breathe. ADopt this PHiLosopHY of course you MIGHT BeGin new exercise plans, MeDitAte More often... BLAH, BlAH, BlAH.

But wHere Are you right now?

Without our FLAWS, FAULTS, and FOIBLES, we would be less lovable— MUCH less lovable.

Treat yourself as kindly as you do your best friend

How kind and understanding we are when we help a friend in crisis, or just in a low spot.

Friend in a low spot

Drench yourself in self-kindness!

Women are very good at shining kindness outward, yet if you ASK how kind they are to themselves, they often cry.

Turn the kindness spotlight inward.

Before we can move to healthier ways, we must be where we actually are.

RADICAL self-acceptance is a connecting, SOFT, slow, and compassionate way of being. We can help each other.

When you see your "sister" beating up on herself, take her weapons away and just hold her.

When you WATCH animals, you see only self-acceptance. Find ways to expand radical self-acceptance in your life. Adopt a friend and exchange stories of self-acceptance. So often, we trade stories of how bad we've been, or are.

Shift the focus.

Describe the ways you learned to accept yourself today—or last week.

I myself, live under siege from the inner critic, the judge, and the "pusher." I'm studying these selves of my personality and giving them new jobs. Far away

I wish for all of us more radical self-acceptance

Succulent Wild Women can be rich with self-acceptance.

nourishment from the inside

Let us as women be thankful for hearty appetites! Allow us to feel true hunger.

I see so much self-imposed starvation among women— myself included. and then we hide away and eat our hearts out....

The language of cake:

"Oh just a tiny slice!"
"Please— the smallest slice you can cut."
"I'm being so bad!"

Or, a marvelous woman I met, who said:

"I eat cake for breakfast. I know I'm going to want it all day anyway, so I just start with it."

Michelle

Don't we deserve to eat?

How Do you nourish yourself? (Besides Food)

nourishing touch?

nourishing WALKS?

nourishing BooKS? You Are The Book

nourishing words? SATISFACTION surprises Deeply delicious WISDOM loving learning Hope Kindness

nourishing naps?

nourishing self-TALK? You Are so Deeply loved

The nourishment starts on the inside. When we tell ourselves and others the truth and identify WHAT we really want and need, we Are nourishing Ourselves.

SATISFY your Hungers For:

· Spirituality   WHAT Does yours look Like?
· intimate Connection   How Does it Feel?
· creative expression   Are you Free?
· Physical Movement   can you Move?
· Conscious Breathing   let Breath HeAL you
· Being of service   How?

Women Are often nourishing others, and need to practice More self-nourishment.

Keep taking your inner nourishment pulse. Notice the tendency to leave your self.

How is your inside nourishment?

♡   How Does it look inside you?

WHAT MAGAZINES Tell US

- THAT Size 12 is BiG.
- THAT We MUST Dress right, or end Up in A "Don't" Column.
- THAT We MUST Constantly seek perfection.
- THe SAMe information every Month with Different titles.
- How To COOK, eAT, Dress, BeHAVe, and think.

I reAD 50-60 MAGAZines every Month. Many of these Are "WOMen's MAGAZines." THere is an Astonishing AMount of information in these MAGAZines. Some of it is informAtive, supportive, and reveAling. Much of it is repetitive, negAtive, and DeMeaning.

I reAD MAGAZines pArtly to Feel Connected to other WOMen. WHen I reAD the letters to the editors, I Feel Like I know these WOMen, thAT we're on the SAMe wAvelength.

"MAGAZines" thAT FloAT Around in My Mind

SoMe of WHAT I reAD in MAGAZines Feeds My inner Critic: I HAVen't reDuceD My thighs, Shrunk My Dress size, or stopped snAcking Between MeAls.

I want MAGAZines to Be More intimate, Braver, and More collaborative. Many Are Moving in this Direction.

MAGAZines rely on their reADers to Buy and subscriße — let's tell them WHAT we Want to see!

- More ACTUAL-siZeD BoDies
- First person Accounts
- Being more creatively Alive resources
- Celeßration of women As they really Are

THe MAGAZines Are only reflecting WHAT we Don't tell them.

Let's send e·MAiL, letters, and MAKe pHone CAlls to sVGGest, offer, and constructively complain. Let's Fill the PAGes with our reAL selves and FAVLts!

We MUST reMeMBer that MAGAZines Are sKeweD By the "ForMULA." THey Do not reflect our Truth!

SoMe MAGAZines that nourisH Me

FAT

Appetites by Geneen Roth

Getting our Bodies Back by Christine Caldwell

Feeding the Hungry Heart by Geneen Roth

Staying Healthy with Nutrition by Elson Haas M.D.

The Owl was a Baker's Daughter by Marion Woodman

Nothing to Lose by Cheri Erdman

Real Gorgeous by Kaz Cooke

When Food is Love by Geneen Roth

Enlightened Eating by Rebecca Ruggles Radcliffe

The Woman's Comfort Book by Jennifer Louden

The Invisible Woman: Confronting Weight Prejudice in America by Charisse Goodman

Intuitive Eating by Evelyn Tribole Elyse Resch

Breaking Free From Compulsive Eating by Geneen Roth

resources

- Love Your Body Regardless From Body-Judgment to Body-Acceptance By Patricia Lynn Reilly, www.thegirlgod.com/love-your-body.php
- Curvivality Magazine and add website: curvicality.com

Music

- Been Found by Ashford and Simpson with Maya Angelou
- Endless Wave, Vol 1 By Gabrielle Roth

JOURNALING

Journals can provide a pathway to the inner you

Every woman is living a journey of her own life. We are each teachers and healers, and our voices count.

"In our journals we are in search of the real self — of what really moves us, what we really think, what we really feel."
                                        Elizabeth O'Connor

The blank page calls us out to play with pens, paints, glue, lipstick, ink or pencils.

COME OUT TO PLAY!

The journal is a witness, an unconditional friend, a soul teacher. Sometimes, we just complain. Writing out the dark thoughts lessens their power. Having conversations with ourselves in journals gives us chances to work things out in private. We collect and form our own history (and her story) with journals.

I started keeping journals in 1979. The hundreds of volumes are precious to me, and are full of my life and lives.

NOW THAT I write BOOKS, I write in MY JOURNAL less often. I've stopped JUDGING the Quantity of MY writing.

For A long time, JOURNALS were MY only "proof" that I COULD write.

THE PROVING JOURNAL

People WOULD ASK WHAT I DID, and I WOULD SAY, "I'M A writer!" they inevitABly WOULD ASK, "WHAT DO you write?"

When I answered "JOURNALS,"

the precious Journal

SOMETIMES they CHUCKLED or SMIRKED, or SAID, "No really— WHAT DO you write—For reAL?" As though JOURNALS were less VALUABLE someHow.

| JOURNALS Are not less VALUABLE |

WHATever COAXES US out of HIDING, to write, record, and express, is A revolutionary Act. It SAYS that We Believe our Lives count. Our Lives DO count.

I will Always Be thank·full to: MAYA Angelou, Anais Nin, Anne Morrow Lindbergh, MAY Sarton, Colette, Gertrude Stein, and so Many other Great writers, For opening up their Journals, and their Lives, to Me.

It gave me courage to write my own journals and Books.

THANK YOU.

When I look Back in those Journals now, I see clearly that <u>nothing</u> is <u>lost</u>. I'm using words and images From those journals in my current writings.

In 1993, I created SARK's JOURNAL and PLAY! BOOK As sort of A journal guidebook and actual Journal. I Get letters From 8-year-old girls who are Filling these journal pages with their list of "I wants" and describing who they love and why. It Fills my Heart to think of young women and girls playing on B i G B l a n K P A G e s

Instead of Being trapped in Barbie pink plastic diaries with locks — As though they have to keep their thoughts locked up.

Before

I want:

now

I DreAM oF SCHooLS with Journal Classes and HArDcover Blank Books As stanDArD issue

It Doesn't MAtter WHAT you write in A JournAL. It MAtters that it is yours.

"I Began these pages For Myself, in order to think out My own particular pattern of Living, My own individual Balance of Life, work, and Human relationships."

anne Morrow LindBergH

Your own JournAL AWAits you.

JUMP.

WAYS TO BEGIN A JOURNAL

GET A BLANK BOOK, lined BOOK, one with quotes or pictures — WHATever MAKes you smile inside and want to rush HOme to write in it.

TAKE your BOOK and MAKe it yours with photos, Dots, Scribbles, or Just your name (or secret name).

CAreFVlly choose your writing tools so that your words can gleeFVlly leap onto the paper.

Begin writing About anything: the Branch of A tree, A kind cotton Sock, your CAT's pAw, A piece of neglected Fruit, the wAy you curl into sleep, A prayer For your unBorn Child, WHAT you wish you Could SAy, WHAT love looks Like, your wish For the world, the love life of Flies, WHAT kind of Flowers MAke you GASp.

reAD JVLiA CAMeron, NAtalie GOLDBerG, MAy SArton, anne Morrow LindBergH, anAis Nin — There Are so MAny GreAt WOMen writers WAiting For you to reAD them.

Let your Journal Be A Joy For you.

Story · telling

Women tell stories to each other.

We sit or WALK close together, telling stories of our lives, loves, discoveries, challenges, pains, and DREAMS.

stories PASS THROUGH us like streams...

or, as my friend Susan says: "Wasn't it grand to talk about everything—and nothing?"

We can TALK on the PHONE FOR HOURS ABOUT nothing in particular

Stories are our way to illuminate the path and find common ground.

Our illusions of separation disappear when we hear stories of another's struggles or discoveries.

We hear ourselves say,

"I can relate to that!"

in our stories Are seeds of our
Deepest longings and wishes. Through
story, creative Buds can Burst into
Life.

BOOKS Are collections of stories For
everyone to reAD and Find their own
Meaning in. My BOOKS tell stories of
My Life and process. I Believe these stories
Assist people in their creative Growth.
especially women.

A story can TraveL without you and inspire many

"every WORD A WOMAN writes cHanGes
the story of the WORLD, revises the
OFFiciAL version."

CAroLyn See

My story of sitting in A Hotel loBBy
With A siGn thAT reAD Artist Available for Dinner HAS
inspired other
women to venture
out into the world More creatively or
UnUSUAlly.

My story of placing an AD that SAID:

incredible Housesitter seeks incredible House

WHich resulted in A rent-Free Mansion For
2 years, encourAGeD other women to place ADs
or reACH out in new ways.

When I FounD My MAGic cottAGe in San Francisco
By visuaLizing it and Describing it in My JournAL,
it prompted others to visuaLize More.

There Are Many types oF MAGic cottAGes

All the Stories I HAD reAD or HeArD About
these subjects inspired Me—WHich resulteD
in My experiMenting, and then writing ABout
My experiences. WHATever inspires you will
inspire others!

We Are richly connected By our stories

Telling stories through letters, JournAls,
Books, By computer, or on the pHone Are All
WAys to connect with other creAtive souls.

Don't ForGeT your DreAm Life!

Tell More stories!

Your stories can teACH, upLiFt, remind,
Give permission, reassure, inspire, Give
strength, Allow HuMor.

THe tiniest story in your Life can Deeply touch another.

You cannot Know the effect your story MiGHT HAVE.

PLEAse let your stories Be HeArD

"A story is A MeDicine that Greases and Hoists the pulleys, sHows us the WAY out, Down, in and Around, cuts for us Fine WiDe Doors in previously Blank WAlls, Doors WHicH leaD us to our own KNowiNG."

CLArissA PiNKoLA estés

"in WHicH We Are introDuceD to Winnie-the-POOH anD Some Bees, anD the stories BeGin..."

A.A. Milne

Painting

Painting is putting colors from your Heart onto paper. Painting is playing with color. Painting is Dancing on paper

Truth: We need more women to be painting.

So often, we Don't try new forms for fear that it "won't look good." I myself Have produced some of the ugliest paintings ever! Hideous, rust-colored, unidentifiable BLOBS, that I Hurriedly threw Away.

It is so easy to let our inner critic stand over us As we paint, and chortle AT our feeble results. even Before the paint dries, The critic Judges it inferior. Many of us Don't even try to paint!

We wonder if we're A painter — and if we Don't see evidence of prodigy AT A young Age, or Hear an inner calling, we conclude we're not painters. Also, who Are our female role Models? Truth: We can All paint.

Perhaps not "professionally" (unless we want to) But think of All that you Do that May not Be "professional": cooking, photography, running...

You can express parts of yourself in painting that come from nowhere else. There is an interior part of you that HAS no words and Dreams in color.

It is the part that Gasps At sunset sky colors, pauses AT A pine tree Glistening with Dew, and sees the sunlight on A child's Hair.

HOW TO PAINT

PUT YOUR EGO, CRITIC, JUDGE IN A DRAWER.
lock it.
Go on an ART store ADVENTURE. BUY SMOOTH or
NUBBLY PAPER—WHATEVER SINGS to your FINGERS.
TEAR it into ODD-SIZED pieces. BUY ONE BRUSH.
CHOOSE COLORS THAT you love in iNK, WATERCOLOR,
ACRYLIC, OIL or **FINGER PAINTS.**
MIX COLORS RANDOMLY or PUT DIRECTLY ONTO PAPER.
EXPERIMENT. KEEP GOING. MAKE MORE MISTAKES.
LAUGH AT WHAT DEVELOPS. **PUT LAYERS of color
on top of EACH other.** TEAR THE PAPER UP IF YOU
DON'T like it.
Glue the pieces into the center of the next
picture. See if it Develops into anything.
Spill paint onto the PAPER. WATCH WHAT
FORMS next. THIS is painting.
You ARE A painter.

©SARK 51

Perhaps your painting calls for photographs, or tiny doors cut to open, or bits of flowers. Maybe it wants to be a card for your dearest friend, or a page in your journal.

The paint will lead you to new places if you can follow the splashes.

Where do the splashes lead?

Be kind to your new paint spirits— they might be young and unknown. How will you know about yourself and painting if you don't paint? Certainly <u>not</u> from past evidence. That has no basis. Did someone tell you you can't paint? A person, or your own inner critic?

They lie.

Paint your heart's colors! let paint leap out.

Allow your inner visions to be in color

Costumes

Succulent Wild Women wear Costumes.

Costumes can Be:

Outrageous Hats

painted Gloves

and Slippers

Velvet capes

Vintage Jackets with rare Buttons

Decorated Handbags

Unusual Shoes

Handmade jewelry

pieces of BATIK

painted silk scarves

large color-full rings

Wearable toys, tiaras and necklaces made of symbols.

Costumes are a way for women to play adult dress up — we can let different parts of our personalities out to have fun.

One time, I WAS traveLing in Mendocino— A romantic CaliforniA coastal town—and SAW A rare sight:

Six Women on the street, All wearing plastic Groucho MArx Glasses, noses, and HATS.

I stopped to AppLAUD them, and Found out they were 4 Generations of WOMen, playing together on VACAtion. I vecLAred them to Be Succulent WiLD WOMen, and the Great-GrandMother threw Her HAT in the Air and SAiD,

"you BetcHA, Honey!"

THey HVstled off Down the street, Arm in Arm. We Forget to Dress in Bright colors, in our own Distinctive styles.

<u>WHAT WiLL the neighbors Think?</u>

THey'll Think thAt they WiSH THey could HAve FVN too. A5K them! We MUST Wrap ourselves like the Gifts THAT we Are.

Costumes promote Adventures. I used to Go out in the BAHAMAS, in an evening Dress, riding A Bicycle and CArrying A BAMBoo WALKing stick. Then, I'D PARADe through the cAsino Carrying MY stick. You cannot Be lonely THis WAY.

Costumes Are According to MooD. TAKe your temperAture BeFore Going out (or stAying in). WHAT Do you really Want to WeAr?

WHAT speAKs of your SOUL?

SOMETIMES A COSTUME IS A FAVORITE COTTON SHIRT and pants—I HAVE one top I CALL MY nanny top—BECAUSE THAT'S WHAT I FEEL LIKE WHEN I WEAR it.

My MOST COMMON COSTUME is PAJAMAS. I LIKE WHITE COTTON MEN'S, WITH DRAWSTRING pants. SIZE XL FOR ROOM TO DANCE!

I paint MY JACKETS AND SHOES WHEN they BEGIN to BORE ME. SOMETIMES I ruin them By painted "MISTAKES." THESE I CUT UP AND turn into COLLAGES (or SOMETIMES I JUST throw them AWAY!).

I'd LIKE to expand MY COSTUME WEARING AS I AGE. Let's ALL WEAR BRIGHT TOGAS, WILD SHOES, FLABBERGASTING HATS AND MEET IN A DRUMMING CIRCLE, in A FOREST NEAR A HOT SPRING. All COSTUMES WELCOME!

How to Arrange A Succulent WILD WOMAN evening:

Poster size

SUCCULENT WILD WOMEN
DO WILD things!
Meet us for an evening of Delicious FOOD, ABUNDANT LAUGHTER, poetry, and inspiration.

or ✉ reALLY TINY

Send an invitation of UNUSUAL SIZE AND WORDS. include poetry.
"extend Surprising invitations."
SARK

MAKE your invitation Succulent.
Describe events BrieFLY AND with intrigue:
"IMAGINATION FESTIVAL With other Succulent WILD WOMEN, we want you!"

Dress: WILD IMAGININGS, DANCING SHOES.

Food: CHOCOLATE, FRUIT, HOMEMADE BREAD, CHEESE.

Purpose: TO BE SUCCULENT TOGETHER!

Arrange to do one Activity: (or more if the spirits move you!)

· DANCING AT HOME, IN A WILD CLUB YOU WOULD NORMALLY NOT GO TO, IN A SMOKE-FREE, WOOD-FLOORED DANCE STUDIO.

· DRUMMING AT A BEACH BY A FIRE, BY CANDLELIGHT AT HOME, IN A FOREST BY MOON·LIGHT.

· POETRY READING IN A CIRCLE RANDOMLY, IN A GARDEN, AT DAWN.

· JOURNAL WRITING SPEND TIME WRITING TOGETHER ABOUT: love, RADIANCE, YEARNINGS, TRAVEL, ADVENTURE, or SERENDIPITY. READ EXCERPTS TO EACH OTHER.

THERE ARE SO MANY SUCCULENT WAYS TO CONNECT WITH WOMEN. WE ARE ALL CRAVING UNUSUAL, INSPIRING, SOULFUL TIMES.

let's spend
MORE of our Lives
in the
SOULFUL TIMES

MAKING MISTAKES

Creativity is filled with "mistakes." Women are often preoccupied with perfection and miss out on the mistake-making process. We start with a vision in our imagination — then we try to translate it into paint, clay, crayon, pastel, dance or song.

The paint leaps off the brush and a big dot appears on the paper. Is it a mistake? Or a messenger of color, sent to invite us to explore?

 So often, I scribble or color and then judge the result too quickly. I decide it is inferior, or a mistake, or not worthy in some way. Yet the process is a glory if I can detach from the result.

Sometimes while writing a book, I imagine an audience of critics looking scornfully at what I'm writing. I call in my creative and spiritual mentors to "scatter the crowd" and restore some balance.

We need to make more mistakes! As women, and people, and especially creatively. Start more projects! Start more than you can ever finish. Fill yourself overly full so that your imagination spills out. Watch children. So much of what they do is a "mistake" by our narrow adult standards. Women can step boldly forward as working creative people — not just hobbyists, dabblers, and only dreamers.

There is a marvelous organization called Guerilla Girls — they wear masks and appear at museums and art openings to expose the small percentage of women artists showing in museums, and other injustices for women in the art world. In order to have our creative voice heard, we must speak — even if we are unsure about what to say. Dare to make more mistakes! Laugh at perfection!

Your mistakes are treasures, and so are you!

SHARING OUR CREATIVITY

Creativity thrives in solitude — not isolation. As creative women, we need a community.

A creative community stands strong

Julia Cameron has done this so beautifully with her life and works: <u>The Artist's Way</u> and <u>Vein of Gold</u>. All the women doing their "Morning Pages" form a telepathic creative community. Groups have formed that are inspired by these books. Whatever gets us moving, talking, collaborating creatively is a blessing.

So often, creative acts occur alone, and are shared with a few close friends or loved ones, or not shared at all.

We Think We Are Alone

During my 12 years as a "starving artist" I doubted if I would ever be read or acknowledged creatively. Whatever I sent out was rejected, whatever I chanced to share was often misunderstood or judged harshly.

DEAR SARK
WE ARE SORRY
WE CANNOT
USE THE MATERIAL
YOU SENT US...

It was very lonely. I might have grown deeper roots if I'd had a community. I might have been braver about submissions, shows, or collaboration opportunities.

So I created a "community" out of my friends and

loved ones, and relied heavily on their support, insight, and encouragement.

We grow in the company of others

Like plants or flowers

Still I longed for a wider community. I dreamed of living with other creative souls, trading art supplies and inspirations.

Somehow I kept creating. I widened my community by reading and dreaming and using the

The phone connects us all

If we can connect in groups, by phone or e mail, at bookstores, churches, and teahouses, if we can share our creative spirit with other women, we will bloom and ripen and grow.

Find just one friend who likes this idea. Form a creative duo. Check in with each other and start making gentle plans—you can share art supplies!

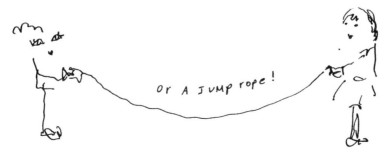

Or a jump rope!

creative expression

THE WAY ARTIST'S BY JULIA CAMERON

BiRD BY BiRD BY anne LAMott

learning BY HeART BY corita kent & Jan steward

A creative companion BY SARK

Life, Paint and PASSion BY Michell's Stewart Cassou Cubley

HArold Purple and The crayon BY crockett JOHNSON

Life's companion BY CHRiStina BALDWIN

Writing Down the Bones BY natalie GOLDBERG

Zen Zen Seeing, Drawing BY Frederick Franck

POeM cRAZY BY susan WOOLDridge

Silences BY Tillie OLSen

Zen ART Writing in The of BY RAY BrADBury

WiLD HeART Dancing BY elliot SOBEL

For Writers only BY Sophy Burnham

The of vein GOLD BY JULIA CAMERON

Write FroM The HeART BY HALZina Bennett

The WORLD of richard STine BY richard STine

WAtercolor For the ARTiStically undiscovered BY THACHer HURD & JOHN CASSidY

resources

- THe Sun—A MAGAZine of iDeAs, A lively literary MAGAZine of iDeAs And intelligent words—www.thesunMAGAZine.org/
- Intuitive Superpowers: De-Mystify & Activate Your Intuitive Life created By renowned intuitive psychotherApist VAlerie TAte. A self-guided 6 module ProGrAm to De-Mystify & Activate your intuitive life. vAltAte.com/intuitive-superpower-course/
- Lee HArris www.leeHArrisenergy.com

MUSiC

- Hit reCorD, hitrecord.orG
  Founded And led By Actor And Artist JosepH GorDon-Levitt, HITRECORD is An open online coMMunity for creAtive collAborAtion. Learn And prActice creAtive skills through fun And eAsy proMpts.

How to explore money

"relax. your money is not your life! it just feels that way sometimes." SARK, (from the poster, "How to relax about money").

Women are exploring money in their lives now more than ever before. Money is beginning to flow into more women's lives as we become more visible, more "of the world." | Money | is | Beginning | To | Flow |

Women have had a long history of money scarcity and the shifting of this is profound. Most new small businesses today are owned by women.

Money can be such a mystery. We need to be able to study its energy, accept abundance, and also learn about the gifts of not having money.

The dance of money can feel all-encompassing, energizing or draining, a curse or a lesson.

Often, women are dependent financially, and afraid to upset any money balance they may have achieved.

I believe that women deserve to be financially compensated for child care and household management— if that is their life situation.

I grew up with a mother who was raised with money, and a father who was not. This created interesting money issues for me. I'm either generous or frugal, and have a lot to learn about the "middle."

Women are frequently in a fog about money— the finite and detailed issues of investing, savings, tax planning, and estate management are something

"For later," "For someone else to do."

The more responsibility women take for their financial lives, the more money will be available to them.

As my business has expanded, and more books have sold, my income has also grown. This has brought new challenges of distribution, planning, investing, and other matters I've never faced. I keep thinking that I shouldn't have to do it all alone. Yet of course I don't, because I have a staff and there are professionals to help. It reminds me of my blocks about math—that girls weren't good at it—so I wasn't.

Women are just as smart about money as any man, and just as deserving to have a lot of it.

I let my blocks about math wall me in...

Women can:

· Study money
· Make friends with money
· Channel money to others
· Accept money
· Step into financial power
· Open up new money makers

Your talents and energies deserve financial reward! Women can open up more to the subject of deserving. We think it's selfish to want too much. We minimize our needs and stifle our own growth.

"Well, I don't need much."

The world hears that and responds accordingly.

STUDY MONEY: Open up the subject in your life. read books about money. Have conversations with other people. keep a money journal about your patterns and habits, successes and weaknesses.

My Money Life

MAKE Friends with money: Find Joy. Full ways to play with money. Stop speaking negatively about it. Encourage Gratefulness for whatever you have.

MAgnify positive Money Feelings.

I AM WEALTHY on the inside

CHannel money to others: practice tithing — A percentage of your income to whatever you Feel is Good or nourishing For others.

Give Money AWAY with no Strings attached. (it can be a tiny amount). Give money anonymously or secretly (the energy increases without your ego involved).

Accept Money: Stop Fighting For the Meal check! Allow others to "Gift" you. Accept presents Graciously and Gratefully.

Open up new Money Makers: Create income "Streams"

income STREAMS

that can Flow without your Direct involvement. This can be in the Form of Dividends, royalties, or commissions.

These income streams can expand with time to Fund other plans you May Have.

Money is Fascinating, Fun, Mysterious, and invigorating.

<u>You can create Money</u>

- WHAT Are your FinanciAL DreAMs?
- How Does Money scare you?
- How Does Money sAve you?
- WHAT can you learn About money?

 Sit with your Money Feelings

We Are not TAUGHT enough money lessons — especially not About creAting money in HeALThy, innovAtive WAys. We need to Be our own teachers and call upon others For Help.

I WAs in A money Group with some Women thAt Felt so power·Full it scAred us and We Quit.

It is now O.K. to Be FinanciAlly successFuL.

I HAve reALizeD thAt my own needs Are FAirly simple, But my vision For The worLD is HUGe and costly.

I envision: (AMong other Things)
- an Artist's and Writer's BAnK.
- The SARK-FoundAtion: providing creAtive support To Artists, CHiLDren and OLD people.
- BrAnD new plAn For Arts in All scHools.
- the unions of nursing HoMes, CHiLD cAre, and Humane societies.
- prosperous liBrAries.

WHAT else? WHAT Are your Glorious visions for the worLD?

We can BUiLD and creATe MirAcles

We can creAte Money

HOW TO FORM A MONEY GROUP

• FIND SEVERAL WOMEN WHO ARE INTERESTED AND OPEN TO EXPLORING MONEY IN THEIR LIVES.

• Meet monthly or weekly if motivated.

• Choose a book to work with (see resources).

• MAKE A TIME COMMITMENT 1-3-6-12 Months or weeks (exploring money will bring up lots of feelings and it may be tempting to quit. Providing some structure will help).

• Choose a facilitator, or rotate each time. one person needs to be responsible to the "Assignment" chosen and manage the time so that the Group doesn't dissipate its energy "CHATTING."

• Keep notes: your money group is revolutionary and deserves recording. You may want to help other women form money groups.

let money be a flying carpet in your life use it to travel to where you want to go

How to Accept power

You Are A power.Full Woman

How Does this feel? Do you embrace it or push it aside? The subject of power isn't explored very much or taught in schools, or even by parents. Luckily, this is beginning to change.

People see me as a power-full woman. Yet, I don't see it myself. Why?

We are endowed with power by our very birth, and then shrouded from the knowledge and acceptance of it. My mother is a power-full woman. When I comment on it, she laughs and says, "Oh no, I'm not."

What do we think power is?

The dictionary says:

"Ability to do, act, or produce," "Great ability to do, act or affect strongly; vigor; force; strength," "A spirit or divinity."

I think we must study power and what it means to us as women. Power means to me:

- Standing strongly in your own center and living from your heart.
- Truth-telling, wisdom, and strength. How often do we think of power?

Think of your women friends.

Identify the ones you consider power-full. Why? What qualities do they share?

How can we increase healthy power as women?
Consider:

- spiritual power
- physical power
- financial power
- emotional power
- psychic power
- healing power
- love power

POWER

In what ways are you power-full? In what ways do you feel less power-full? Do you think of power consciously?

When I think of power-full female role models, I think of:

Athena, Amelia Earhart, Maya Angelou, Sylvia Beach, Mother Teresa, All Mothers, Eleanor Roosevelt, Oprah Winfrey, Elisabeth Kübler-Ross, Bette Midler, Barbra Streisand (there are so many fantastic and power-full women!)

In what ways are you like these women? Different?

We need new definitions of power. It is not "power over" I'm interested in. I think that as women, we think that it isn't nice to talk about power. Or, we think of power as domination. Power needs to be re-visioned for women.

It's time for us to create power, be visible power-fully, and accept power.

I envision a world full of power-full women, who know it and act from it. Imagine the miracles we can create!

Living with Money, Living without Money

My Grandfather was an entrepreneur who created his own income, my father worked for a corporation for 39 years. The differences were striking to me. My father spent 6 days a week traveling during much of my early childhood. I wish he could have owned his own business and been home.

After my 250 jobs, trying to get money illegally, studying millionaires, and living without money for 12 years, I decided to try and live with money.

In 1989, I invented something called "spirit cards," which were handmade art piece affirmations. I created a display for them, and put them in a store. That led to hand made affirmation books, and then inspirational posters.

I made 12,000 posters by hand in my garage, using spray mount, colored pens, and color xerox.

The posters were sold in a catalog and the first one, "How to Be an Artist," led me to write a whole series of 17 more.

How to be an Artist / How to be really Alive / How to really love a child / Cats are angels with fur / Dogs are miracles with paws / How to relax about money / In-spiration Guide / Being a wonder full Friend / Invite someone dangerous to tea

Then my books were published. *visions of posters danced in my head*

I then hired a business mentor to work with me on a daily basis so I could learn about business and create a company that would support my visions and creativity. @CAMP SARK was born in 1993, and vibrantly continues on as Planet SARK in 2022.

I planted an impossible garden, and it's blooming ecstatically

I AM an Author and Artist who is Living my Dream, and owns a company. (the kind of company I always wanted to work for).

I stay at home and work in pajamas. I still procrastinate and get scared.

Here are <u>some</u> things I've learned about Living with money: _I'm still learning!_

- Money doesn't solve all problems. It makes some things easier, and some more difficult.
- When you have money, others may want some. Then you must decide.
- Living with money responsibly must be studied.
- Money can act as an insulator and separate you from others.
- People can get jealous and judgmental about your money and how you choose to spend it.
- Living with money can cause fears of living without money to resurface.
- Hoarding, cheapness, extravagance, poor planning can all sabotage.
- Money guilt can occur.
- You might have money, and your friends might not. How is that?
- Sharing money is more complicated than it seems.
- Money is really fun and can provide outstanding environments. What happens in those environments is still up to you.

I'm
in
my
pajamas
more
than
I'm
out
of
them

Fun
money

157

My parents were always worried about my not having money during my years as a starving artist. Then, when I got some money, they worried about what I was going to do with the money!

Here are some specific ways I lived without money, and my recommendations for those who wish to try:

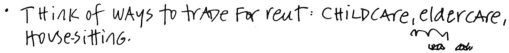

• START A "Dinner tree" where you ask a different friend each night to share their dinner with you. 7 friends = 7 nights.

The Dinner tree had plates in the branches

• Develop an appetite for simple foods.

• Think of ways to trade for rent: childcare, eldercare, housesitting.

• Use the library a lot, books will nourish you.

A good thick book filled her up

• Spend lots of time walking outside — it will physically refresh you.

• Devote yourself to some art — you won't notice poverty as much.

• Refuse to be shamed by poverty or be judged by society as inferior.

• Ask for help. Develop your humility.

Stand on top of a tall hill fling your arms wide and shout,

"O.K. I owe everyone!!!"

- risk owing people.
- realize that you can choose to create money.
- study money as an energy.

Creating Money Sanaya by Roman Duane Packer

- realize that many of the great artists, poets, and spiritual teachers were poor.
- live your dream and realize that the money is important, but incidental.
- invest in your [self] your dreams, talents, and abilities.

YOU ARE WORTHY OF INVESTMENT

- live as powerfully as you are able without money—develop your spiritual gifts.
- read about people who didn't have money: <u>A Tree Grows in Brooklyn</u> by Betty Smith, <u>Hunger</u> by Knut Hamsun, anything by Henry Miller.
- concentrate on learning to love your self.

MAY YOUR MONEY CHOICES COME FROM YOUR HEART.

Money and Power

Creating Money by Sanaya Roman & Duane Packer

Transforming Your Dragons by Jose Stevens PH.D.

Visionary Business by Marc Allen

Money Meditations for Women by Jo Ann Lordahl

Your Money or Your Life by Joe Dominguez and Vicki Robert

I Could Do Anything If Only I Knew What It Was by Barbara Sher

You'll See It When You Believe It by Dr. Wayne Dyer

Do What You Love The Money Will Follow by Marsha Sinetar

Seven Laws of Money by Michael Phillips

Creative Visualization by Shakti Gawain

Max Makes A Million by Maira Kalman

resources

- Prosperity Pie by SARK
- overcoming underearning by Vicki Robert
- Wild Money by Luna Jaffe

Isabel

I first saw her in Big Sur, in the patio of a cliffside restaurant. She was sailing through, wearing wildly painted leather shoes, a very bright white blouse, and her white hair swept elegantly on top of her head.

I said to myself, "there's my new friend!" Then, I was struck by shyness and couldn't get up to meet her. An hour later, I saw her in the parking lot, getting into a big car with her women friends. I knew then that I had to meet her— and rushed over to give her a copy of my poster "How to Be an Artist."

She beamed at me, stopped and read the poster out loud, in its entirety, in her New Zealand accent.

She then said,

"Why don't you give me a call in Berkeley, dear!"

When I first visited her, she flung the door open, looked intently at me and said,

"My dear. Come in and lie down immediately! You look very nappish."

She brought me out to her marvelous garden, and I laid down on a brightly colored mat in the sun.

She then brought me succulent bits of food on tiny plates. I said to her,

"Isabel, may I ask you a personal question?"

"Well yes, I hope it is personal!"

"Were you ever married?"

She replied impishly, "No, I escaped that particular thing."

Isabel owned a sportswear design company and had her own factory for 22 years. She traveled in "high society" and had famous mentors. Yet, she doesn't speak of herself very much or often—you must be patient to find things out about her. She is consistently curious about other people and their stories.

Her home reflects her taste and style and is filled with flowers, bright colors, fabulous artwork, and simplicity.

Isabel is one of the wisest souls and youngest spirits I know. Once on a trip together, I found her on the balcony outside our room, with a flower in her hand, peering intently down. I asked her what she was doing.

"I'm looking into the hearts of flowers with this magnifying glass. Come see!"

A whole world is inside the heart of a flower

Her approach to life is one of "fresh mind" and alive choices. Isabel gulps life.

She is also rather mysterious and quite reserved. She says she was raised by the "last of the Victorians."

162

Isabel can so graciously decline an invitation, you don't even realize for awhile that she's said no!

One time, I rented a house on top of a mountain in Big Sur for my 39th birthday, and invited Isabel for brunch. During the night, the rains had washed the roads out, and people coming to the party were digging their cars out of muddy ditches by the side of the road. People were also calling to say that they wouldn't be coming due to the weather. All of a sudden, there was Isabel, who had driven her 1968 Plymouth Fury right up that washed out mountain road! She swept in with a big smile and basket of fresh muffins.

To Isabel, everything is brand new and the world is a wonder.

Once my friend Brigette was in a car with Isabel and suddenly Isabel called out, "Oh look! Succulents!" Brigette thought she was talking about succulence, but Isabel had leapt out of the car to greet the succulent green plants she had spotted from the car window.

Isabel most definitely lives juicy!

"Not for me the pale shades of anonymity, but the hot lush colors of imagination, creativity, and accomplishment."
Isabel

Adrienne

She came to interview me for a column she wrote, and as soon as I saw her, I yelled out,

"Oh! I just love you already!"

Her face and essence had completely captivated me. When I first heard her laugh, I knew we'd be friends forever.

Adrienne is beautiful, funny, irreverent, talented, sexy, and quite outrageous. She is also driven, highly sensitive, relentless, and a perfectionist (did I say stubborn?)

She sat in the magic cottage in my hanging chair and said I should meet her boyfriend. I thought, "Oh no. He won't be her equal, and I probably won't like him."

The moment I met Ken, I felt a rush of love that continues to this day. (And he is very much her equal!)

Adrienne's love relationship was a model of the kind of relationship I wanted one day — romantic, honest, deeply loving with lots of play and humor. I read poetry at their wedding.

I watch closely as Adrienne practices "intimate negotiations" and transparent sharing of feelings. I marvel at her ability to share her feelings — they just float out — raw, sometimes edgy, and in the moment.

She doesn't question our friendship and its strength to hold feelings. This gives me strength.

When I met her family, I named them "Functional Family Camp." At dinner, her father asked everyone to join hands and speak about how they were feeling!

Later I said to Adrienne in a jealous moment, "You're so lucky. Your parents are so great!"

Her eyes darted,

"They weren't <u>always</u> this way!"

They had been in therapy and worked on, and are working on, their issues.

Then Adrienne and Ken had a baby named Zoe and asked me to be godmother. They are an adopted family for me.

I've learned so much soaking in the very real glow of Adrienne. Her realness and flaws inspire me to share mine (she's saying "WHAT FLAWS!?").

I wish everyone could know Adrienne, which is one of the reasons I'm writing about her here. Her spirit is very bright and will and does travel far. She is a writer and has much to say — motherhood, intimate partnership, friendship.

She was the creative director of our company, CAMP SARK and we created SARK's Magic Museletter and a multitude of other magical creations together.

The succulence of Adrienne is profound and affects my life everyday.

Giselle

SHE HAS WILD UNRULY RED HAIR THAT STICKS OUT everywhere and SHE DOESN'T HIDE HER CRABBINESS. Giselle REMINDS ME OF PIPPI LONGSTOCKING— ALL GROWN UP. (REMEMBER PIPPI? GREAT CHILDREN'S BOOK CHARACTER).

Giselle is an OLYMPIC WEIGHT LIFTER. ONE OF HER AMERICAN RECORDS is FOR THE <u>SNATCH</u>, WHICH SHE WILL TELL YOU WITH A DEVILISH GRIN.

SHE ALSO DESIGNS AMAZING CLOTHING AND SCARVES, WHICH ARE SOLD ALL OVER THE WORLD. HER loft SPACE is FILLED WITH LOOMS AND BEAUTIFUL WOMEN HELPERS WITH NAMES LIKE VENUS.

JUST HEARING ABOUT HER SCHEDULE EXHAUSTS ME, YET I'VE ENJOYED A TIME WITH HER AND HER ENDEARING HUSBAND EARL, SPRAWLED ON PILLOWS IN FRONT OF THEIR FIREPLACE. WE ROASTED MARSHMALLOWS, AND TALKED ABOUT everything AND NOTHING (SHE LIKES THEM LIGHTLY TOASTED).

SHE HAS THE ABILITY TO WORK DEEP, AND RELAX DEEP. IT'S A GOOD COMBINATION.

Giselle is very LITERAL. WHEN I CALLED TO TELL HER THAT I WAS PUTTING HER IN MY BOOK, SHE THOUGHT I MEANT ADDRESS BOOK! BEING AROUND Giselle IS A REFRESHING EXPERIENCE. THERE IS VERY LITTLE CHATTING OR SMALL TALK.

Giselle is one of the most direct, sometimes abrupt, women I've ever met. It shocks me. One time I said,

"I've missed you," and she replied,

"Why? We hardly ever see each other."

Her tone was calm and simple and makes me realize that many people don't just "say it straight."

I explained my theory of being telepathic friends to Giselle—where you speak on the phone or just telepathically, without making plans—I don't think it's a familiar way to her, as her way isn't to me. Yet her directness is invigorating to me and you can tell where you stand.

Giselle is quick, penetrating, funny, eccentric, endearing, and very wild in spirit. She is open, animated, and deep.

She is also prone to outbursts and sudden angers that can seem alarming, until you know her heart is good. Just knowing Giselle is definitely a wild succulent experience! (and her mother Harriet is awesome).

Giselle is a woman who inspires courage and physical action. I am so glad to have a character like her in the world.

Marjorie Elaine Anderson Kennedy

My mother is a succulent wild woman. She is the "SARK" among her friends.

She was in the Marines, and was the first female cigarette representative in the midwest. In her 20's, she lived in a boarding house in San Francisco, and demonstrated steam irons in the window of a hardware store. She used to walk near the cottage I live in now, over 50 years ago, and dream of living in San Francisco!

A sore wisdom tooth led her back to Minnesota, where she met and married my father, Art.

Her commitment to family gave me a lot. She was there everyday and managed the kids and house with a small income and no car, while her husband traveled most of each week as a salesman.

She was imperfect and made mistakes. She also initiated going to family therapy in the early 1960's. She talked fairly openly about our family problems when most of her friends didn't.

I've often thought that if we'd had a really good family therapist, we could have resolved, or at least uncovered, the sibling incest and other problems that were so devastating to our family.

Still, there was love, and I named my mother

"Marvelous Marge" and now her mail comes addressed to her that way!

Dear Marvelous,

Sometimes when she isn't so marvelous we call her "Marge the Sarge."

My mother can be intimidating and intense. She is also prickly, controlling, and extremely opinionated (it's scary to write about my mother's flaws).

When I called to ask her if I could include this portrait, and confessed to being nervous about her reading this book, she said,

"Susan. I told you a long time ago. You write what you need to, for _you_. Not for me or what I think, or what anyone else thinks!"

After soaking in these words, I said,

"Thank you. I also need to confess that I've been the recipient of you having strong feelings about things I've written, which you hoard and then attack me later with!"

She laughed. "Yes. I suppose I do do that. But you're just going to have to learn to ignore it!"

And so, I shall.

When I asked my mother what she is most grateful for, she replied,

"Elastic!"

My mother also knows how to, and has, hypnotized chickens.

169

Women's Friendships

Some of my greatest, deepest, most gloriously intimate friendships have been and are, with women.

I have also felt horrified, afraid of exploring the dark side, and unable to practice fair fighting—or any fighting—with my women friends.

There is such rich terrain to explore in women's friendships. All or most of us have mothers, and often we project our unresolved mother issues onto our women friends.

My particular method was to: leave when it got ugly. Sometimes this is good. Sometimes there was more to uncover that could have created a better resolution and ending. "Nice girls" don't fight. Yet not fighting ended almost every friendship I had that developed problems.

One or both of us was so afraid to go into the darkness together, to speak our truths and to describe our experience.

These truths would have been oxygen—some of my friendships ended by suffocation.

I tried to pretend everything was "just fine"

I would be so afraid of losing a friend that I didn't tell the truth, and would lose her anyway.

We strike unconscious bargains with our women friends. One of mine was: I won't tell the truth if you won't leave me. This worked well as a vicious cycle.

vicious cycle

I've learned very piercingly How the unspoken can Deprive A Friendship of real nourishment. THe timing of that speaking is crucial.

Telling A Friend you Dont Like Her BoyFriend early in their relationship, or later if she HASnt ASKED you, can Be lethal.

repressing anger is common among women. We Fear the outcome if we express it — yet repressed anger turns poisonous and ends Friendships.

let your anger out in responsible and conscious ways... eventually, yet soon

My Friendship History and style HAS TAUGHT Me A GreAT DeAL, and the lessons I've learned HeLp Me in My current Friendships.

My First Friend WAS named Missy. She lived next Door WHEn I WAS very young and HAD lots of sisters and one Brother. This WAS A Fantastic world to Me — All these siblings — I only HAD one Brother. I remember Moving Away From the neighborhood When I WAS 11, and Thinking I WOULD Die without Missy. i DiDnt Die, But i sure Missed Missy!

My next important Friend WAS in High scHOOL. Leigh CHALLENGED Me, WOKE Me up early and invited me out to Play in the world. Thank you Leigh!

My college roommate is still A very DEAR Friend. SALLy WAS the Most Grounded Friend ID ever HAD, and We Also Hitch Hiked All Over TAMPA together, cAusing commotion During college.

After college, there WAS Julie. We were "Best Friends" For Many years, and in some WAys, that Friendship HeLped Me to truly Grow up. Bless you Julie

When I moved to San Francisco, I had a ten-year friendship with Helen. Helen was my first real adult friend. I wish we'd learned to fight and resolve conflict—perhaps our friendship could have continued.

My women friends now—Adrienne, Susan B, Brigette, Nancy, Robin, Tori, Joe, Eleanor, Diana, Elizabeth K, Vanessa, Isabel, Elissa, Vimala, Angela, Cecilia, Debbie E, Susan H, Kathryn, Katie, Nicole, and Debra are all contributors to my health and sanity and support me by telling and hearing the truth. I love them each dearly.

These circles of women are power. Full

I believe that these circles of women around us weave invisible nets of love that carry us when we're weak and sing with us when we're strong. Let's lean back and let the arms of women's friendships carry us and help us to know ourselves better, and live our lives together.

- Who are your real friends?
- Do their faces light up when they see you?
- Are they able to celebrate your successes?
- Do you tell each other the truth?
- Do you have ways to resolve conflicts?
- Do you need more friends?

How do women's friendships nourish and support you?

Are you a marvelous friend?

How to Make Friends
(At any Age)

Go out: This sounds obvious, but sometimes we forget that in our homes, the chances of making new friends is rather slim. Although, you could try neighbors, mailpersons, children. You could invite them in— "import-a-friend!"

Change routines: Our habits can insulate us from new people and experiences. If we go somewhere new, we might meet someone new.

Take a brand new path

Be available for friendship: People will not know that you're interested in friendship unless you indicate it somehow. A smile, a comment, an invitation, a phone call, a note, are all good ways.

welcome to the neighborhood we love it here!

Join something: It doesn't matter what you join— you could meet someone who could be a friend.

Redefine friendship: There are so many kinds of friends. Shopping friends, carpool friends, game playing friends, phone friends, club friends, computer friends.

meditation friends

invent new kinds of friendships

of various ages

See where you could use some more Friends, and then find some!

Change your Attitude: We all want friendship, yet we all experience friendship scarcity. Being a good friend to yourself will encourage others to want to be friends with you. Create a grateful, receptive attitude even if you don't always feel that way. It is easy to blame others for friendship failures. The failure is usually with ourselves.

Be Brave: Finding friendship can sometimes feel scary and vulnerable. We all have memories of rejection. Be your most courageous self.

Be Ageless: Consider making friends outside your own age group. Often, people of different ages can be good matches in energy and interest levels.

Be inventive: See if someone dining alone wants to eat together. (My mother recently did this with great success. She said to me, "Wasn't that a succulent wild woman thing to do?") Yes, it was! You can gently and intuitively give new people chances to include you. Try it.

Remember: Give someone the gift of being friends with YOU!

174

Portraits of Succulent Wild Women

AT 70 BY MAY SARTON

ain't I A WOMAN! edited by Illona Linthwaite

eARTHLY PARADISE BY colette

embracing our essence BY susan skog

THE DIARY of Anais Nin edited with an introduction by Gunther STUHLMANN

THE HEART of A WOMAN BY MAYA Angelou

WOMEN MAKE the BEST FriENDS BY Lois Wyse

THE seasons of women edited by GLoriA morris

DANce of anger BY Harriet Lerner PH.D.

THE Girlfriends Keepsake Book BY Carmen renee Berry and TAMARA TrAeder

I SHOCK MYSELF BY Beatrice WOOD

Girl FriENDS BY Carmen renee Berry and TAMARA TrAeder

resources

- THE MARGINALIAN.
  MARIA POPOVA SAYS "THIS IS MY ONE-WOMAN LABOR of love, exploring WHAT it MEANS to live A DECENT, inspired, substantive life of purpose AND GLADNESS."
- MY GRANDMOTHERS HANDS BY RESMAA MENAKEM
- THE HILL WE CLIMB BY AMANDA GORMAN
- PLEASURE ACTIVISM: THE Politics of Feeling Good BY Adrienne MAree Brown

Succulent Wild Woman Groups

Groups Are A Great Way to "Dance with your Wonder-Full Self" in the Company of others! They can Be very spontaneous and informal, or More organized. Here Are some types of "Groups"

- Phone Group: I HAve entire Friendships That take place on voicemail. My friend Susan and I leave 5-6 Messages at A time For each other that are like little radio programs. We save them and listen with A cup of tea when the mood is right. You can Also provide support and encouragement on the phone By reading quotes or poems, remembering special dates, or making "support calls" to each other.

A friendship that dances telepathically on the phone lines

- Activity Group: Succulent wild women Are excellent company. Having tea parties, Going out to wild Dance clubs, reading succulent Books, Moonlight Hiking, and Grown-up slumber parties Are some ways to expand your pleasure options. It's like Having A Bank of people you can Draw interest on.

- Food Group: Succulent wild women love to eat! and could share Favorite restaurants, delicious food, and Fascinating conversations. Women can Be such nourishment for each other.

They sat at separate tables and had inspiring conversation

MAKE and DESIGN new money with women and color on it!

- MONEY GROUP: SUCCULENT WILD WOMEN Are rich and can share their knowledge of inner and outer wealth. You can practice techniques to DRAW money to you, or to learn How and Where to share it and to make money SAFE, fun, and relaxing!

- CREATIVITY GROUP: SUCCULENT WILD WOMEN Are curious and have creative appetites. Meet at MIDNIGHT, FULL MOON, with JOURNALS and sleeping BAGS. GAther in DRUMMING circles, painting classes, or sculpture GARDENS. Bring SKETCHBOOKS to a playground. Hire MAle models to pose in A DRAWING SALON AT your Home.

FULL MOON DRUMMING JOURNAL PLAY

Invent your own Group and FORMAT. Here is A list I use For SARK GAtherings of Succulent Wild Women:

the reMARKAble Susan

1. everyone is A STAR (MAKING and naming STArs)

2. Circles of ecstAsy (stories of ecstatic moments)

3. Journey into the DARKNESS (JOURNAL and ARt to find treasures of the DArk)

4. rADICAL self-Acceptance (How to experience more)

5. Fresh love (Giving it to ourselves/others)

6. WILD iMAGininGS (JOURNALING/SHAring entries)

7. "I want" exercise (writing/ARt to List wants)

8. CREATIVE VALIDATION (WHAT is it? How to Give/receive it)

9. SPLENDIDLY imperfect (lists, ADMissions, Acceptance)

10. MicroMoveMENT support (How to Begin/continue)
    Tiny Little STEPS

11. EATING MANGOES NAKED (and other SUCCULENT ACTS)

12. invite someone Dangerous to teA (WILD teA PARties)

THeir teA CUPS FLOATED ABove the tABle and STEAM DevelopeD FACES

IF you WOULD like to receive A Free Glorious Guide to Begin or leAD your own "SUCCULENT WILD WoMAN" Group, PleASe visit PlAnetSARK.coM/SWWGroups.

I'm currently recovering FroM A terror of Groups and Always AvoiDeD theM. THen I JoineD one thAT is HeALING, FUN, and very GroUNDING.

WoMen Meeting in Groups creAtes an energy thAT is very power-FULL. PleASe explore the possibicities of More Groups in your Life — I send you new energy For it!

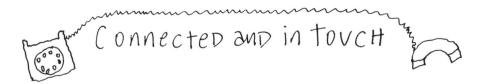

Connected and in Touch

"Stay in touch!" "Let's have lunch!" "We'll have to get together soon."

We all toss these phrases around because we genuinely want the connection, or we don't know what else to say.

Women are infused with niceness to the extent that they don't tell the truth about connection.

It was easier in kindergarten. You could just point to another girl or boy and say "let's be friends!" and you were.

We all have different levels of energy for friendship at different times. If you don't feel an honest friendship response, set the <u>woman free to make another friend</u>!

Being passive-aggressive can be rampant among women. Listening to phone messages that are draining — out of obligation, promising to "have lunch soon" when you don't really want to, avoidance, "white lies," and doing activities out of fear, obligation, or guilt are all examples (<u>F</u>ear, <u>O</u>bligation, <u>G</u>uilt spell FOG. Don't do it!)

If we can all promote truth-telling with women seeking connection, there will be plenty for everyone!

We've all been in both positions: seeking and being sought after.

Here's a possible response to someone seeking when you would rather not continue or expand the connection.

"Thanks for asking me to ———. I need to be honest and say that my availability for friendship right now may be different from yours, but thank you for thinking of me."

If you can practice this in your own language, and until you feel comfortable saying it, you will add so much to the integrity of your connections.

I used to feel that I had to connect somehow with everyone who asked. I now see that it was related to my lack of boundaries, desire to merge, and fear of judgment. (of course sometimes, I just didn't like the person!)

Now I remember this when I am seeking connection, and if it somehow isn't working out with the other person, I try not to take it personally.

I invest in a source that's more ripe.

note: sometimes I fail in this attempt and feel rejected!

Serendipity is a good indicator. When serendipity is at play, there is an effortless quality to connecting. When the connecting is an effort or struggle, sometimes it is a sign to let go, or at least loosen up.

Check with your body. It knows almost instantly if the connection is a good one.

There are so many excellent women to know! Find the nourishing, inspiring, endearing women. Hold them close. Cup their little faces in your hands and say "You are good and adorable! I like you so much!"

WAYS TO SHARE SUCCULENCE
WOMEN SHARING SUCCULENCE IS A JOY!

We Are All Givers, and can Also Allow our receiving Abilities to Grow Wilder.

◉ SHARING SUCCULENCE can Be:

- Getting A White cotton shirt and Writing A Tribute to your Friend on it.
- Dedicating your phone Message to A Friend For A day— or A Week.
- MAKING or sending an anonymous Book of poetry.
- Assembling A Book or collage of Her AMAZING qualities.
- Setting up A "Mystery Date or trip" For You and A Friend.
- offering to WASH Her Hair.
- Sharing clothes you Don't normally wear.
- letting A Friend read your Journal.
- Going on A "Miracle WALK" and Hiding treasures Along The WAY for your Friend to Find.
- Meeting For A picnic and HAVING surprise Friends there.

◎ receiving Succulence Can Be:

- Asking For Keen listening—no solutions.
- Allowing A Friend to clean your scary Drain. (thank you Brigette and Susan!)
- opening A Book to your FAVorite pArt and letting yourself be read to.
- Daring to say "WOULD You rub My neck?" no reciprocation.
- MAKING A list of WAYs you enjoy receiving.
- MAKING A list of WAYs you Block receiving.

let your Giving inspire your receiving. reAlize that we cannot truly Give without receiving.

WHAT is succulent in your Life that you want More of?

Ask 3 Friends to cAll you 3 times During the DAY and leave you Messages of things they Like About you.

I cAlled All My Mother's Friends and sAid "lets not WAit until My Mom Dies to say WHAT WE so loved About Her— WOULD you pleAse tell Me now?" I then MADe A Book of WHAT they sAid. She treasures this Book.

We need to express our Most succulent selves— sooner, Deeper, and More often!

Mentoring

OUR TREASURES MUST BE SHARED. MENTORING IS A WAY of creating A laboratory or A tiny community in which succulence can grow. ~ *it can grow into A magnificent flower*

Do you remember informal mentors early in life? one of mine was Cecilia. She was old and lived alone, and seemed to love it. I went to her house and presented theatrical monologues that I would write and perform. I remember her acceptance of my essence and how safe I felt there. *I also remember plate-sized chocolate chip cookies and trays of African violets on the windowsills*

One of my writing mentors was my 5th grade teacher who loved what I wrote and encouraged me to write more.

My 1st grade teacher, Mrs. Gooler, was my library and reading mentor. She inspired me to get a library card and read a book a day. She would also send me to the 5th grade class to read out loud to them. *visions of books danced in my head*

My grandfather was my traveling mentor. He encouraged me to keep a journal on trips and then read my writings to him when I got back.

Miriam was my art/life mentor. She bought my original artwork at inflated prices and advised me on my "pattern of living."

Now in my 40's, I am a mentor for others — through my books, and more personally with younger friends.

Mentoring is a superb way for women to share energy and gifts, to teach rituals and traditions, and to

Assist others in living more succulent lives.

"WHAT IS A WEED? A plant WHOSE virtues HAVE never BEEN DISCOVERED."

Emerson

All women can Mentor, if they wish. We All HAVE specific talents, wisDOM, and knowledge to share. we forget that we can so strongly affect others, JUST in being who we Already Are.

Mentoring creates opportunities to continue succulent circles of women. especially if we choose not to pArent, it's a way to let our gifts continue on.

Meditate on Mentoring. See if you feel inspired to take action, or just give others the opportunity to learn from you.

I've been in a reciprocal Mentoring relationship with VanessA since she was 11. she is now 17. I Definitely learn As Much from Her As she might From me.
(it's very inspiring for me to realize that I was not this evolved At 17)
A GOOD sign for the Future!

VanessA is a MArvelous COMBiAation of electricity, Genius, and splendiD iMperfections. She lets me read Her JOURNAls sometimes, and I feel blessed to be Able to see WHAT Grows inside of Her.

She is the Best preview I know of for an upcoming succulent wiLD WOMan. MAy All of our young women Stand so strong, Brilliant, and BeAutiFUL.

Growing As Wild Women

We must insist on succulence! Our lives Are too rich and rare to have less. We will grow more As we practice.

Growing can be uncomfortable, loud, unfamiliar, and feel perilous to our underdeveloped personality selves.

Growing As wild women involves breaking out of cages, boxes, stereotypes, categories, and captivity. It involves standing tall, laughing loudly, and being who we really are.

> "I've Always wanted to cultivate modesty But I've been far too busy."
>
> DAME edith sitwell

Growing means separation from: being victims, passive-aggressive participants, unwilling caretakers, lying lovers, fake friends, or "nice girls."

Growth means change: change your attitudes, perspectives, patterns, and habits.

Succulent wild women are inside All of us. We can invite them out to play! ←

Growing means letting go of: WHAT others will think, of narrow possibilities, of tight clothes and uncomfortable shoes. Growing means: Accepting power, telling the truth, creating miracles, and making the most Alive choices.

yes

Succulent wild women are all around you. Look for the bright eyes, ready smile, and unusual clothes. Or perhaps it's a more shy succulent wild woman who dresses and appears more quiet, and then you get close enough to bask in her succulent glow.

There are so many fabulous Wild Women! Here are a few of my favorites— famous and more obscure. Please continue the list by adding your particular favorites. Our naming of these women is very important. It creates channels for others to discover them. We must remember our succulent wild women!

Dame Edith Sitwell. Elsa Gidlow. Beatrice Wood. Isadora Duncan. Sarah Bernhardt. Ruth Gordon. Gertrude Stein. Martha Graham. Miriam Wornum. Jessica Tandy. Anaïs Nin. Jessica Mitford. May Sarton. Anne Morrow Lindbergh. Dame Sark. Imogene Cunningham. Maya Angelou. Madeleine L'engle. Emily Dickinson. Colette.

WHO can you think of?

Draw out the wild women—in yourself and others.

We were born to be wild, I assure you.

Just look at our bodies—wild containers for our great big hearts.

I love you.

It is now lusciously 2022

Come with me in my time transporter!

It acts like magic to travel through some highlights of the last 25 years of my life:

SARK's MAGICAL TIME TRANSPORTER

First, I've eaten lots of food.

I've cried a lot of tears, laughed really hard, and loved sleeping and napping, and of course LOVING.

all of these are very important

I am now 67, or as I like to describe age, "level six." I've lived a LOT of my dreams, resisted lots of others, and feared many things that did not happen.

somehow I kept going

I wrote and created many beautifull books, and designed colorfull products and life-changing programs. I teach and play in what I call the marvelous messy middle-where I welcome all the feelings in my emotional family.

i don't always like them

I'm learning to love them

Letting go of a lot of my resistance to feeling my feelings has allowed me to enjoy life so much more.

I've made so many mistakes and done things badly.
I'm sure you have too.

MISTAKES HAVE BEEN SOME OF MY GREATEST TEACHERS.

I love what the artist Beatrice Wood said:
"My life is full of mistakes. They're like pebbles that make a good road."

There are countless ways to ride on the road

I have ACQUIRED SOME WISDOM ALONG THE WAY, and you probably have too.

I believe that we gain wisdom by the living of life—with an open mind and an open heart—and with curiosity and a willingness to truly learn from our mistakes.

I want you to know that the Spirit of SARK is part of everyone.

It's the part of you that is Wildly Loving, Succulently Alive, and Full of Frisky Fun, Terrific Transformations, and Daring Dreams.

YOUR DREAMS ARE VERY RESILIENT AND WILL WAIT FOR YOU

And of course, the SARK Spirit includes your fears, despair, worries, sadnesses, and hopelessness.

THESE ARE NOT AS POPULAR

Allowing all your feelings to simply be as they are, and you being willing to feel them, is part of building what I describe as MENTAL WEALTH.

Love Never Dies

In these last decades, death came as a mighty teacher: my parents, older brother, and beloved cat Jupiter. Those losses initially flattened me. Later I came to understand they contained much more than they took away.

I believe that there can be surprising gifts in terrible things, and that it's important to feel fully the loss before trying to find any gifts.

some people try to skip to the gifts

The most recent mighty loss was my former beloved fiancé John, who died in my arms in 2016 after a terrifying diagnosis and nine months of illness.

We had just published our first book together and had planned to create so much more.

When we first met, John told me he was qualified to adore me, and I discovered that he really was!

Dr. John Waddell was a psychologist devoted to the possibilities of the human spirit. We met in 2012 on a metaphysical cruise in Alaska, and when he asked me why I was still single, I replied that I had married myself in 1997, and didn't yet know how to include another person.

he showed me how

In the 4 succulent years we had together, John's life and love filled me beyond eternity. Once when I told him that I felt ashamed, he said, "oh, Susan. I'll hold the little hand of shame with you."

I knew then that I wanted to marry him.

John helped me learn to love all the most unlovable parts of myself, and I'm still discovering more, and practicing loving those too.

i also found out that I was qualified to adore him

He radiantly said to me, just before he died, after I asked him how I could possibly go on without him,

"Susan, you get happy. Happier than you've ever been. And when love comes again, you go full speed ahead."

I was grieving so DEEPLY after John left. I didn't see how I could possibly be happy, much less happier than I'd ever been.

It wasn't just the physical loss of John that felt devastating, it was the loss of all our dreams and the incredible life that we had lived together.

I discovered that grieving is not something to get out of, it's something to get into—and that my happiness could be found in the grieving, not separate from it. I had felt so afraid that if I really went into grieving, I would never get out.

i created paintings about how I felt and what I was learning

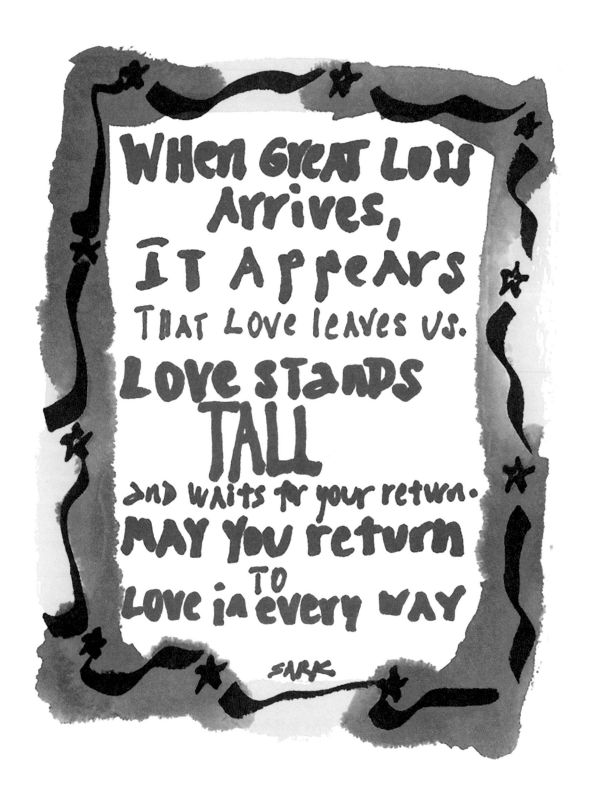

WHEN GREAT LOSS
Arrives,
IT Appears
THAT LOVE leaves us.

LOVE STANDS
TALL
and waits for your return.
MAY You return
TO
LOVE in every WAY

SARK

Deeply Grieving, Wildly Living

So I practiced deeply grieving and wildly living at the same time. Doing both gave me buoyancy and an understanding that life could be good, or even enriched, with the grieving—and not permanently ruined by it. I opened myself to wildly living by asking for and accepting invitations, and I chose to do new activities that would have previously made me nervous. I found new courage and happiness by doing those things.

there are many miracles in the new

let's do more of the new more often

There's just no way to get out of the grieving. I couldn't leave it behind, as much as I wanted or tried to. So I took the grieving with me. It felt like I needed both deeply grieving and wildly living to be able to fly—they operated together like bird wings.

i did this for years

I REALIZED I WAS MOSTLY HAPPY BEING SOULFULLY SINGLE AT THAT TIME, AND I DECIDED THAT rATHER THAN try tO FIND one PERSON tO LOVE, I'D stArt DATING THE WoRLD.

I resolved not to wAit to love, BUt to immerse myself in love And in loving.

First, I wrote A BiG FAt letter All ABOUt it And PUBLISHeD thAt on my MAGIC BLOG. I Announced thAt I WAS GOING on A love ADvenTure And WAS COMMItteD to experiencing my life DifferenTly now. I explAined thAt I HAD Been recently reADiNG All the poetry in my HOUSe while lying UPSIDe DOWN to Give myself A NEW VIEW.

I Also shAreD HOW My HeArt WAS OPeniNG in thAt letter:

"I'M reAWAKeninG my rOMAntic HeArt slowly And more DeliBerAtely now. I'M Allowing it to Drip like HONey. I'M trusting Divine timing more thAn ever BeFore."

I received CASCADes of responses from people inspired to Do the sAme thing.

The Upside Down Page

READ THIS PAGE UPSIDE DOWN TO SHIFT YOUR PERSPECTIVE.

I PRINTED IT THAT WAY TO REMIND YOU THAT YOU CAN
CONTINUALLY CHOOSE TO SEE THINGS DIFFERENTLY.

THIS IS WHAT I WANT US ALL TO KNOW: THAT

love comes again,
like lava creates new land

SOMETIMES IT MIGHT TAKE A VERY LONG TIME AND MIGHT
LOOK DIFFERENT THAN YOU EXPECTED, OR IT MIGHT NOT COME
THROUGH ANOTHER PERSON AT ALL.

Love might come through an animal
or a dream fulfilled
or your own rhapsodic self

I BELIEVE THERE IS A NEW PARADIGM OF GRIEVING
AVAILABLE TO US, WHERE WE DON'T WAIT FOR SOMEONE TO DIE
to practice the art of simultaneously grieving and loving.

Living THIS WAY, EACH LOSS AND PAIN BECOMES PART
OF THE POWER OF THE DEEPLY COMPASSIONATE, RESILIENT,
AND UNSTOPPABLE PEOPLE WE BECOME AS SUCCULENT,
WILD, AND WISE WOMEN.

AND, IN MY STORY, ROMANTIC LOVE DID COME AGAIN!
REMEMBER MY BIG FAT LETTER ABOUT DATING THE WORLD?

Love Comes Again

A remarkable soul named David read my letter and left a message on my Inspiration phone line (415-546-3742). He thanked me for writing that letter and for living the way I do. He added, "I just love your heart. This is how I live too, loving the world."

A new sort of Love vehicle

And then in one breath he exclaimed:

"I love you, I love you, I love you, I love you, I love you, I love you, I love you,

I love you, I love you, I love you, I love you, I love you, I love you, I love you!"

(And then he paused and asked:)

"Is this too much?"

(Then his message continued with the same passion:)

"I love you, I love you, I love you, I love you, I love you, I love you, I love you!"

i gasped at the audacity

Hearing the love in his voice caused me to risk calling him back. We talked and communed deeply and laughed wildly for hours on the phone that day and every day for the next three months, and we built an incredible bond based on our mutual spiritual practices and commitment to joy.

DAViD AnD I sHAreD Our vulnerABilities AnD sHADOW PArts, supported eACH OtHer As we nAviGAteD CHAllenGes, AnD let Ourselves Be truly seen, Known, AnD loveD.

A succulent WilD WOMAn frienD Of DAViD's HAD tolD Him tHAt He is liKe A MAle version Of Me. AnD He is. He HAD MArrieD HiMself Before KnOWinG tHAt I'D Done tHAt AnD written ABOut it, AnD He Drew ColorfUll, inspirAtionAl "siGns Of love" AnD put tHeM up All Over His HOuse As A spirituAl PrActice–AnD Built A life BAseD on fAitH.

I experience HiM As An AnGel Of Love WHO Also DOes tHe Deep AnD Often unCOMfortABle inner WOrk Of AlCHeMiZinG tHe terriBle AnD WOnDerfull tHinGs.

We joineD Our lives toGetHer in SAn frAnCisCO in ZOl8 AnD Are nOW life-lovinG "full speeD AHeAD" PArtners in love, life, Business, AnD CreAtive projects AnD teACHinGs. We Are BOtH writers AnD visionAries, supportinG AnD inspirinG eACH Other, AnD sHArinG Our love AnD teACHinGs witH tHe WOrlD.

DAviD is A succulent WilD MAn, AnD Our union Of love HAs expAnDeD My HeArt forever.

Loving And Being loved like this HAs increased my CAPACity to receive more love. MAny women, me included, Are often Better Givers thAn receivers, And I'm prActicing the Art of receiving now As much As Giving. I invite you to Join me.

you'll know thAt you're prActicing if you feel uncomfortABle ;-)

The Union DAvid And I shAre is significAntly helped By the commitment we've mADe to one mAin vow in our relAtionship:

We eAch tend to our own Alignment first.

We fill our own internAl cups, rAther thAn coming to eAch other hAlf-empty, trying to Get filled. This hAs resulted in us Being ABle to Give more often from the overflow of love, And to keep creAting A mAgnificent loving relAtionship thAt is reAl And rooted.

We Are Also seeing A GreAt therApist to Guide us.

i AlwAys sAid I wouldn't ever Be in Another "unsupervised" relAtionship

Tending to our own Alignment first requires exquisite self-cAre.

Miracle Methods

I'm a longtime self-love activist. I've developed foundational spiritual practices and primary habits to excavate early traumas and help myself heal, so that I can truly LIVE as a succulent wild and wise woman.

I also think of these practices as Miracle Methods— because they are so miraculous in my own life.

A FABULOUS NEW FRAME

It is miraculous to me that I can mostly* live my succulent wild life so joyfully, no matter what circumstances occur.

*i say mostly because it's an art to practice

Any wisdom I've acquired has come through my lived experiences.

I've had the privilege of sharing my practices with people at transformational events and healing centers around the world, and in my private mentoring practice and online courses.

I'm honored to see how they assist people in rising up to cause positive change in their lives, and help create nourishing new ways of being and loving for themselves, and for this world. Here are abbreviated descriptions of the three main methods I use and teach:

1. Connect with your intuition and let it guide you

I call my intuition my "inner wise self", and it has guided me brilliantly since I experienced abuse in my childhood. I later began cultivating my connection to this part of me by turning within and writing what I call inner wise self love notes, from my inner wise self to me.

This has created the most marvelous relationship. I now ask my inner wise self about everything in my life, and the answers I receive are astonishing. Asking is like a miracle.

asking creates miracles

You can create and deepen your own relationship with your intuition in less than 3 minutes, by writing your own inner wise self love note to yourself. You can receive so much love and great guidance simply by asking.

your inner wise self loves to love you

I've written all my books with the guidance of my inner wise self, and I run my life and business with its wisdom.

i still sometimes forget to ask

2. Your inner feelings need to be cared for daily

I was raised to not talk about my feelings. This did not make the feelings go away :-)

Feelings Dial

I've learned that when you can allow your emotions to be seen, known and loved by you—instead of denying, avoiding, or repressing them—you can feel them and move forward. You will then be able to more consistently be loving to yourself and others.

Feelings know only how to feel, and will respond instantly to your naming and acknowledging them. In addition to a deeper process I teach, I practice what I call the 5-second inner feelings care method. Simply say, "Fear, I see you, I hear you, I acknowledge you." Or, "Sadness, I see you, I hear you, I acknowledge you."

This way, your feelings know that you're listening and will tend to them.

This gives them the love and attention they are seeking, and will allow them to soften, change shape, and receive your love. Once your feelings have changed shape, they will move more easily.

i practice avidly every day.

3. Transform your inner critics' dialogue

I spent many years of my life being berated by inner critics. I've learned that the messages we hear inside our heads are meant to be supportive. Any parts of us that are critical are seeking our love and understanding— although at first it certainly doesn't seem that way!

re-assigned.

I discovered that these parts of us are not bad or wrong—they actually think they're protecting us. They just need our guidance and direction. And by communicating directly with these parts, we can learn to decipher and transform their critical messages.

I call this process the inner critic one-step. First I write down all their accusations, and then my intuition and I reply to each message with affirmative and loving counterstatements.

Once you are willing to listen and give them your skillfull attention, you'll be able to integrate all the parts of yourself and experience yourself as whole.

i'm still learning to integrate all the parts

CReAting MentAl WeAlth

As A result of applying these methods, I'm enjoying my life now more thAn ever.

I hAve successfully (mostly) MAde life-Affirming choices And adopted life-chAnging HABits to upGrAde My MentAl And PHysicAl HeAlth over these lAst DecADes.

It's like

And i'M consistently prActicing-except when I'M Avoiding or resisting

In ADDition to tAking eArly Morning long WAlks in nAture, I ADDeD in WHAt I cAll "tiny yoGA" And reluctAnt MeditAtion. All of these Help Me to feel Better More often.

usinG WorDs like tiny And reluctAnt Help Me resist less

often, I resist DoinG thinGs thAt Are GooD for My MentAl And PHysicAl HeAlth. I HAve FounD thAt if I cAn stArt tinier, I stArt More often-And this HAs leD to All sorts of GooD thinGs, And excellent results.

MicroMovement Miracles

I invented a practice I call MicroMovements—it's about creating momentum by more easily beginning. I make the beginning of an activity fun or amusing, which makes starting and continuing so much easier. Sometimes I write single movements, or I might draw a MicroMovement wheel to write 8 at one time. Writing down the movement engages my mind, body, and spirit.

For example, if I want to clean a messy room, I might write: "Open the door to my room and scream. Then close the door."

Almost always, this leads to my actually cleaning the room, rather than just thinking about it or resisting doing it.

Patterns can be JOY.fully rewoven

I've used this same MicroMovement for years to begin and continue writing each of my books:

"Find my lucky purple pen and put it next to my chaise lounge."

Then guess what? Writing actually happens, pages assemble themselves, and books get published.

> even a walk outdoors is helped by
> something tiny like
> "put my tennis shoes by the door"

Beginning more easily is as much about a micro mindset as it is about actually doing MicroMovements.

Being willing to think about how a task or activity could be easier or more fun, and how we can move in these smaller ways, creates a habit of completion, rather than a habit of never starting.

> Whatever it is, do a tinier version

Creating Sweetnesses

One of the best health decisions I ever made happened 6 years ago. I released myself completely from eating any refined sugar. I'd struggled with an addiction to it for many years—my body couldn't process it, and I could never eat it moderately.

i wish I could

I tried so hard to be someone who could just eat a little bit at a time, but then before long, I would "hear" the sugar calling me from inside the cupboard.

it would say hypnotically, "You know you want to"

Yes

and

Yes

I felt like I was constantly either planning to eat sugar, eating it, or recovering from eating it. This pattern felt exhausting, and was a detriment to my physical and emotional health. My doctor told me I was prediabetic, and moving toward diabetes. Even though the amount of sugar I ate wasn't always that much, I still felt under its spell.

maybe you can relate

Poet and psychologist Marion Woodman inspired me with this:

"The longing for sweets is really
a yearning for love or sweetness."

So, I freed myself from constantly seeking sugary "treats" and snacks, and learned new ways to treat myself by consciously creating sweetnesses in my life. And it turns out that my body actually loves whole foods.

Once I learned that I didn't need to eat sugar to feel happy, I started experimenting with what actually feels sweet to me, like: indelible kisses, extensive self-hugging, clean sheets, sudden spontaneous naps, voluminous reading, seeing babies' bare feet, eating mangoes naked, admiring flowers that make me gasp at their beauty, seeing slants of sunshine, soaking in lavender baths, and anything at all to do with kittens.

Now my energy stays more constant—there are no crashing feelings or tiredness from having eaten sugar.

i am so glad

My emotional life has responded so well to these changes too. I'm experiencing less anxiety and finding a more consistent calmness that I'd always wished to be able to feel.

And when I don't feel calm at all, i do my feelings care!

I'm inviting you to give yourself the gifts of releasing anything that is blocking your happiness and succulence.
Whether it's a substance like sugar, a habit of being hard on yourself, or something else that makes you feel bad—you can practice changing it.

in tiny or larger ways

Turning the Perfectionist Dial Down

In order to support my healthy changes, I've also recently made adjustments to my work life. I'd been frequently prone to overworking and pushing myself to do more—the whole "over" word applies often to my experience:

    overdoing, overgiving, overfunctioning, overpromising, overcommitting, overwhelm

    Now I'm practicing doing less in new ways. I use my intuition to guide me in living more of a life that I love, and I actually listen to the guidance and act differently as a result.

    i still often resist the guidance, which is hilarious considering the great results i receive

    And guess what? I've found out that no one notices or says anything when I do less!
    Or do things imperfectly. Or do them in a way my perfectionist thinks is imperfect.

    which is many things

    I've practiced turning my perfectionist dial down from a previous standard of 10 to a 3, 4, or 5, and it's all been surprisingly good.

    I've discovered that I'm much happier when I'm more present with what is, and focus on how much love there is to experience rather than perfection to achieve.

CLOCK OF FORGIVENESS

Yes

no worries
Go without me
Actually, I don't feel like it
it's O.K
nap
sleep

it's O.K.
GO BACK to sleep
call later
nap

Quit

Sing A Song of Surrender leave Your BAGS Lift Your Self UP

Surrender

I know how fascinating the baggage can be... you can still put it down

I wrote these words to support us All in Growing And Glowing:

"The opposite of old is not young.
The opposite of old is new.
As long as we can experience the new, we will gloriously inhabit all of the ages that we are, And welcome all of the dreams that we have."

What NEW Are you creating?

COMPASSIONATE INCLUSIVITY

We Are MADE to Be AWED By life, Filled With wonder, living in celebration And sharing our joy. Simultaneously, we Are Being Called to Alchemize pain And suffering, Be Compassionate witnesses For each other, Challenge injustice, learn About And encourage diversity, And Make real Changes- And Be inclusive in our living of life. It is WHAt we Are Built For, even if we Don't Know How.

According to Oxford Languages, inclusivity is:

"the practice or policy of providing equal access to opportunities And resources For people who might otherwise Be excluded or Marginalized, such As those who have physical or Mental disabilities And Members of other minority Groups."

We CAn learn AND CHANGE even if we Feel scared

We can create New patterns

"Life is HArD. After All, it kills you."

-KAtHArine HePBurn

I love this quote. It MAKes Me lAUGH, And inspires Me to CreAte the new And to sPArkle. I live My life, As MUCH As possiBle, By Greeting wHAtever life BrinGs-As often As I CAn-with GrACe And HUMor. And wHen I'm not ABle to, I use My own PrACtices to fill Myself BACK UP.

Here's HOw I PrACtice sPArkling wHen thinGs feel AwfUl:

◎ Stop foCUsing on sPArkling And turn to Seeing And FeeLing
◎ TAke tHAt Mixture And turn it into Being
◎ TAke exquisite CAre of Myself, wHiCH incLUdes sPeAking so kindly to Myself-And to the PArts of Me tHAt sometimes feel so BAD
◎ Ask for HeAling MirACles, And exPAnd My vision to Be ABle to see And receive them
◎ Allow other PeoPle to HelP Me, esPeciAlly if I think I'M so indePendent
◎ HelP others wHen I HAve enerGy, And Use love to GenerAte More enerGy And More sPArkles
◎ Let love And lovinG leAD
◎ Be still And let the BeAUty come

MAny thinGs CAn Be MAde Better By A nAP And A snACK

Calling All Spiritual Alchemists

During the last 25 years my purpose has remained the same: to be a transformer, an uplifter, and a laser beam of love, in order to help people heal and grow by alchemizing their pain.

As I write this, we are experiencing a global pandemic; catastrophic events as a result of climate change; military conflicts and refugee crises; deep divides in our beliefs; a powerful demand for racial and social justice, equality, and true accountability; and the collective deep grieving for it all.

there is so much to grieve

We are also experiencing a time of increased compassion, technology miracles, expanded human consciousness, significant creative uprisings, and extraordinary innovations.

there is so much to appreciate

There Are so mAny terrible And wonderfull things HAPPening At the sAme time.

I Believe thAt we MUST All BeCOMe spirituAl AlCHeMists, working to Blend together the terrible And wonderfull things into A BrAnd-new HeAling mixture, And then spreAd thAt mixture As FAr And wide As we CAn.

As FAr And wide As we CAn

How Do we keep RISING UP As succulent Wild WoMen with All our love, strength, COMPAssion, And wisDOM?

By reMeMBering thAt we Are not Alone And thAt we Are truly interDePenDent. We Are All DeePly ConneCteD to eACH other.

Declaration of Inter-Dependence

WE Are willing TO FALL down from the WEIGHT of Life and let ourselves FEEL it All— and we will not stay down no Matter WHAT Happens

WHen we FEEL FLAttened, we will let someone know and Accept uncommon kinds of HELP without worrying THAT we AutoMAtically owe anything in return

WE will Lift other women As we Are rising. We will reach back to Help when we can— and Go Beyond where we have HeLPed Before

WE will remember THAT True wisdom is TAKING exQuisite care of ourselves first, so we can Take Better care of others and our planet

WE will recognize REST As A sacred Act and spread The news

WE will remember to SHAre our Succulence and our Love, As we envision A Brilliant Future for everyone, not only The people WHO Are close or FAMiliAr To us

WE will educate ourselves About privilege in All its Forms, and dedicate ourselves to equity and inclusion. When we dont know How To change, we will Admit to not knowing, and Then stay committed to Finding ways To change anyway

WE will SHAre our Abundant JOY and Creative Dreams As an uprising, and Be A W i LD inspiration To This world

WE will join with The Many women who Are Now Be-ing and Be-coming more of Their True selves Than ever Before, As we All SuPPort each other and expand into our Fullest Power

Circles of Women

I First wrote the words on the next page in 1997, And Have lived them As much As possible ever since. And they're even more true today. May these words nurture And support us As we move Forward in the next 25 years And beyond, As the Succulent, Wildly Wise Women we Are being called to be.

214

Love to All readers of SARK!

andrew + Jennifer Oliver + kitties + Mr. Films

andrea Ben + nico

Arline + Barry

Alexandra + Zeus

Edward + Vladimir

Emily Claire

Kathryn Bennett Roberts

leslie Lewis Savilla + Christian

Amy, rob Bee Evie rose + animals

annie kyle + Alice

Alan + Nathalie

Arnold + Damon

ida rose rotman

Clissa rabellino + spirit of Leo

Linda + russ

Shiloh + Jonathan

Adrienne Ken Zoe Oliver

andy + Janna

Brigette Schoer

A Mighty Thank you to All my friends, Family, Family of choice and every kindred spirit I Love you

David Lee rotman

Patricia Huntington

Peggy Fitzsimmns

andy + Ben

Clark Tate + Tula

Ben + Maddy

spirit of diana Martinez Bleth

Deborah + Lloyd Lloyd

Jennifer + Suzanne Jude + John

Rachel Awes Ben Sam Abe

dr. John Waddell

Cliff + David + Mo

Jonah Elan Tate

Janice + John

Jacquelyn + Artichoke

Ray Davi

Robyn Posin

Susan + Will Mr. Lucky + Missy Moon

Susan Zerner

Tana + Paul

Vanessa Carlisle + Max

Vonda Marlow + Bodhi

Jenny + Maggie spirit of Lucy

Carolyn Hinman

Mnaic reasor

wes + Judy roberts

Virginia Bell

Yofe + David

val + eric + Harper

Meg Baker + Katie Gathels

Michon Javclosa David + Arius

Katie rushing

Jamie Barone

special Thank you to Toshna

anjali

laurel + wes

All neighbors

every heath care professional

kate + Joel

Paola Acuna

Maryann Naples + Debra Goldstein

you reading this

THANK YOU FOR BEING Succulent!

COME PLAY WITH ME!

lots of MAGIC FOR YOU

Big FUN + PLAY

All ways LOVE ♥

I MADE YOU A super succulent MAGICAL KIT!

→ WHAT's in the Kit? *look at the pots*
planeTSARK.com/succulent

super SUPPORT for succulence

it's free! it's yours

Gorgeous Guidance

A Color-full + succulent MAP

GO: planeTSARK.com
You'll find my BOOKS, ART prints, products
FAbulous courses and FUN!

COMMUNE: FACEBOOK·com/planeTSARK → I Love our
@ SARKify Life IG MAGIC! supportive communities
SARK'S MAGIC BLOG Sign up at planeTSARK.com GIFT included

CALL: inspiration line, A Free phone line I've offered
For ALMOST 30 YEARS. I record A 3 Min outgoing message
LEAVE Me A Message if you wish 415·546·3742